Ships Afloat in the City

SHIPS AFLOAT IN THE CITY

FRANK LEDWITH

ROBERT HALE LIMITED
LONDON

© *Frank Ledwith 1977*
First published in Great Britain 1977

ISBN 0 7091 6161 1

Robert Hale Limited
Clerkenwell House
Clerkenwell Green
London EC1R 0HT

Printed in Great Britain by
Clarke, Doble & Brendon Ltd,
Plymouth

Contents

1

An Odd Job

I have enjoyed my work. 'There is nothing better for a man, than that he should eat and drink, and that he should make his soul enjoy good in his labour.' That quotation is, I think, out of copyright. It is from Ecclesiastes, an author not much read by the majority of people, and for all we know maybe as old as King Solomon himself.

For forty-eight years I spent most of my working time in St Mary Axe, a crooked little street in 'The City', the financial centre of London. Here I stayed, from the days of sloping desks, high stools and coal fires of 1924, until the clacking telex machines and long-distance jet travel of 1972, and while many of the little buildings around were torn down and replaced by towering office blocks.

I have sketched those forty-eight years in my book *Ships That Go Bump in the Night*. These notes cover different matters, but it may help to summarize again here my personal background.

I arrived straight from school as a junior clerk or 'office boy' in what was then a small family-controlled firm of a peculiar kind. The firm managed a group of mutual non-profit-making insurance companies for shipowners, controlled by the shipowners themselves. The principal risks covered are 'third-party liabilities', the claims which the shipowners have to pay to other people for damage to persons or property, plus many contingent risks—anything from a man falling down a hatchway to oil pollution, fires, and the removal of wrecks. We call this protecting and indemnity insurance, and shipowners call such a mutual insurance association a 'P. and I. Club'.

Usually, when I say that my job was marine insurance, people look exceedingly wise and say, 'Ah! Lloyd's.' I tend to reply, 'No.

Not Lloyd's. We insure the things which Lloyd's find too difficult.'
I once said this, rather provocatively, in the presence of John
Ridgers, a former chairman of Lloyd's, that unique institution
whose thousands of underwriters pledge all their possessions as
security for risks insured by their syndicates. He observed, 'More
or less true, Frank, but you will agree that Lloyd's helps to make
it possible for you to do it.' Fair enough. As do other insurers, firms
like mine share out the major risks over the whole market, Lloyd's
underwriters in London and insurance companies in Britain and
many other countries.

But the little business which I joined in 1924 is today a substantial one. I finished as second senior of sixteen partners, and the
firm then insured the liabilities of over 20 per cent of the world's
shipping. It is a specialized field, but any organization which can
handle between one fifth and one third of the world market for
its speciality, and hold it for a score of years, has achieved something.

I was lucky to be in such a fascinating business. Both insurance
and the shipowning industry which we served are highly international. We did (and do) business with some seventy countries,
and I travelled to many of them—Australia, India and Japan,
Iceland and Yugoslavia, Thailand, Aden, Malta and Gibraltar,
North America and all over Europe. But most of the time was
spent in St Mary Axe. At different times I did nearly all the jobs
in the office, first running errands and sticking stamps on letters,
then keeping the account books, filing, operating the telephone
switchboard, later conducting directors' meetings, underwriting,
the investment of funds, and most of all dealing with all the
problems which shipowners can encounter all over the world.

In general, I learnt my trade the hard way, by trial and error.
Though I had priceless training from seniors who were masters
of the craft, they believed in giving responsibility to anyone willing
to take it. I was a fairly headstrong person, so I found a good
many opportunities to make mistakes, and thus to make progress.

One of my ebullient colleagues amused himself by creating
nicknames for people. Dawson Miller, the senior partner, formerly
a lieutenant-commander, Royal Navy, was 'The Admiral'. His
brother, a war-time pilot in the Royal Air Force, was 'The Air
Marshal'. A small but very able man was 'The Nipper'. One day

he said, 'D'you know what I call you, Frank? "The Tiger", because when there is a problem, you're always on the attack.'

To look back, as I did in *Ships That Go Bump in the Night,* brought sharply into focus an event which was a clear watershed in my life. After that point the streams consistently flowed in another direction. The event was my first contact with the ideas commonly referred to as 'Moral Re-Armament'. These ideas are well known in Britain and most countries, thanks to the hundreds who have given up careers to work to make them known, and more to the thousands in all sections of society who have accepted them for themselves and applied them where they live and work. The principles are deeply embedded in the Christian gospel (though sometimes neglected) and not unknown to the other great religions. The two most important are the conviction that moral standards should be absolute—honesty, purity, unselfishness and love, and that every person can receive daily guidance from what Christians call the Holy Spirit, humanists (I suppose) call conscience, and Mahatma Gandhi called 'the Inner Voice', provided one is committed to listening for and following any guidance received.

Such ideas were a shock to a young man, a somewhat turbulent and pig-headed young man, trying to make his way in business. Absolute honesty, for example, may be a remote ideal for many. Its daily practice by a person can be rather startling to him and others. I hasten to say that in this field, as in business techniques, I found ample opportunities for mistakes and failures—and still do. But to accept such standards meant a different basis for living from that which I had in earlier years.

It was, of course, not just a personal matter. One of my first convictions was that, if my fumbling attempts to follow these principles produced such a change in me as they did, a multiplication of change in even a few thousand people could radically improve society. To anyone who retains any hope for the future at all, the implication was clear. I was equally bound to spread these ideas, in any natural way which presented itself.

So, in 1972, when my bowler hat came off its peg in St Mary Axe for the last time, I could look back on a business life with two main features. The first was a crowded and varied experience of practical work. I had been part of a good-sized group of men and women, many of them strong personalities, operating a complex international business. It was common for me to switch my mind to a new subject, perhaps every few minutes. It was natural, if ships collided or blew up or whatever, to sum up a situation quickly, and take steps immediately to investigate, safeguard, and so on, perhaps in several different countries. And it was necessary, too, to cope with men of any country, different abilities, and very different outlooks.

To give one example of my work : two ships collided in the English Channel. One was the Swedish tanker *Johannishus*, which caught fire, and many were killed. The other, the dry cargo ship *Buccaneer*, Greek-owned, was insured partly with us, partly with Lloyd's and English insurance companies. She abandoned her voyage to the U.S.A. and put back to Rotterdam for repair. The Swede was taken to a French port by tugs of a French salvage company, and later back to Sweden for major reconstruction.

The first steps, of course, were for care of the survivors, including those injured, then for the safety, inspection and repair of the ships, and an enquiry by lawyers into the causes of the accident. Soon afterwards we had to decide major legal issues, on which would depend liability for claims totalling millions of dollars. Basically it was a question of which country's courts would decide the legal issues, and where would guarantees be given for the claims. It could be in the Netherlands, where our ship (the *Buccaneer*) was repairing, or in France, or in Sweden, or in the country whose flag the *Buccaneer* flew (Liberia, I think). The trouble was that in each country the law was slightly, or substantially, different from the others, and, since there was also the unknown factor of how the court selected would apportion blame between the two ships, it was hard to forecast the result of a choice.

This produced a second difficulty, a division of opinion in what might be called the *Buccaneer* camp. Physical damage to the ship herself and part of her collision liability were insured with Lloyd's and the English companies. Her other liabilities were insured with my firm. The Greek shipowner and I wanted one course of action, Lloyd's and the companies wanted another. They thought the United States courts would favour their interests. If they were thwarted, they might make difficulties about paying claims under their policies. In the end, I told the shipowner that he must decide himself, and I would support his decision. (My firm was the biggest individual insurer.) He decided to follow the advice of his lawyer, with which both he and I agreed, and he accepted a proposal by the Swedes that the English courts (being neutral and internationally respected) should have jurisdiction, but that certain Swedish rules of law should apply.

Before my Greek friend made his decision we were invited—I might almost say summoned—to a conference with the other insurers. We must have looked an oddly assorted trio as we strolled up St Mary Axe towards the library at Lloyd's, where we were to meet. Chris, the shipowner, was short, upright, with a bristly moustache, and his progress was led, as it were, by a well-filled waistcoat and a jutting cigar. Reggie, the solicitor, was a long lean strip of humanity, six feet and five or six inches, with a long lean face like a good-humoured bloodhound, and enormous ears. At that time I still had a little grey hair on top, but not much, was nearly six feet tall, no beauty, horn-rimmed glasses, a pugnacious-looking prognathous jaw and a scarred nose, and slightly overweight, even for my naturally solid build.

At the meeting with the other insurers we found ourselves in a very unpopular minority, but when the matter was finally settled a year or two later all paid up without a murmur. Presumably events had satisfied them that the shipowner's decision was right.

The case thus involved intricate legal questions and also difficult negotiations with both 'friends' and 'foes'. Such a case was not unusual, but for every big and complicated one, there were many which were routine.

The other major factor developed from the event I referred to earlier, and was the aggregate effect of spending some time in quiet meditation with a pen and notebook each day for some 14,000 days. If one reads the Old Testament (valid for Jews and Moslems as well as Christians) one might be pardoned for thinking at first that guidance comes only in stunning forms and arresting words, like the Ten Commandments. There is, however, also the 'still, small voice', and the truths which emerge into one's consciousness bit by bit. It could be said, too, that the sheer discipline of the daily time of listening is necessary to develop one's personality. 'God gave man two ears and one mouth. So why don't you listen twice as much as you talk?' The fact is that I, at any rate, am a very limited and imperfect instrument for the purpose of understanding what must be an infinite plan and purpose, embracing the known and unknown universe, and every detail of everything in it.

Still, one does what one can. Some impressions emerge of what 'guidance' may be assumed to be. One is of a steady, continuing purpose. There are certain recurring qualities. Harmony is one, variety another. There is an expectation of change in the individual, and opportunities for this to happen. (I think of the times I've been prompted to apologize to people. It always goes against the grain to do it, and usually has an effect greater and better than I expect. I think also of the thoughts to do things I considered beyond me.) Another constant urge is to work together with others, and to help them. Above all, there is a certainty that there is a greater framework, a plan for mankind and for me, and that I can learn as much of it as I need to know.

2

How Ships Hit the City

The City of London is many things. One thing is that it is the centre of world shipping. For two thousand years or more, ships have come up the Thames to lie alongside the warehouses, the offices and the taverns—galleys, carracks, hoys, caravels, clippers, steamers, motorships. A few still pass between the lifted roadways of Tower Bridge to discharge and load in the Pool of London, although most of the cargo handling is now done far downstream.

Figuratively, however, the ships come into the City today more than ever before. They sail down its streets, and send their wakes surging down corridors and into offices. In the old days, whenever an anchor was dropped or a line thrown ashore in the Pool or in the docks an eddy of activity spread out through the City's streets. Today, its activities are as directly and almost as quickly affected by the ships which load the logs floated down the Ganges or the West African rivers, the vast tankers which swallow such volumes of crude oil from underwater pipes off the shores of the Persian Gulf, Libya, Nigeria, or Gabon, or the container ships which shuttle their great boxes between all the more developed countries. The oil which fuels them may have been bought in London, the insurance which protects them arranged in London, the money which financed the operation found in or through London, the very trade itself and the arrangements for carrying the cargo linked up in London. There is no monopoly in any of these things, but London is the biggest single centre for them.

And, of course, when something goes wrong, there is a strong chance that people in London will be involved, including people in jobs like mine. The variety of things which happen to and around ships is astounding.

There is a novel by M. P. Shiel which describes how a great sailing ship, carrying a full cargo of sugar in bags, struck a submerged object whilst carrying all sail at night. The inrush of sea water was so great that the crew barely managed to escape overside with a boat or two and anything else which would float, whilst the ship, still before the wind, sailed on, deeper and deeper, and disappeared. Months later, she was encountered, still with all sails set, back on the surface, travelling with the wind without a soul on board. A nice piece of salvage. The cargo had gradually dissolved in the sea (and eventually, after pumping out, the sugar bags were found lying in regular rows on the ballast in the bottom of the holds) and there was enough air trapped under decks to bring the ship, freed of her cargo, back to the surface again. What a marvellous fantasy by that writer whose style was as original as his wild imagination! But in a footnote Shiel said that the incident was taken from real life. This actually happened to a particular ship in the nineteenth century.

I dealt with an astonishing range of shipping matters myself, tragedies and comedies, mysteries and disputes, and in the office I read or heard about many more. When I was a filing clerk, we still had in our files the logbook of a ship which escaped from the Mont Pelée eruption in Martinique in 1902, when a large part of the population of the island was killed. As the hot ash rained down on the decks, this steamer put out to sea. Eventually, the captain ordered everyone below decks except himself, since everything which could burn began to burn, even the wood sheathing of the deck. Somehow, he clung to the steering wheel and kept control, although the lower parts of his feet were actually burnt away as he stood.

A near tragedy which happened in my early years in the City occurred when a British cargo vessel struck the reef of a coral island in the Pacific, and foundered. She was a smallish general trader, a 'tramp' ship, and owned (I think) by the Reardon Smith Company of Cardiff. The crew managed to get ashore, only to find themselves in a trap. There was no water supply on this uninhabited island, and virtually no food. Worse still, they found that the coral reef surrounding the lagoon had no gap in it. They were completely ringed off by coral rocks and breakers. The radio distress call sent after the ship struck was heard, but the ships which came in response could only cruise helplessly outside.

Then, someone had an idea, and one of the native whalers from Samoa (if I recall it rightly—I write from a fifty-year-old memory of the papers) was loaded on the deck of a steamer, with its crew of eight brawny oarsmen, and brought at full speed to the castaways. Three times, in trying to pass the reef, even these men capsized their boat. The fourth attempt succeeded, and they were in the calm lagoon. A few at a time, the weakened crew were brought out, by heroic efforts by the boatmen, and all were saved.

We were involved because, if the crew had been left to die, the shipowners would have paid their families compensation under the Workmen's Compensation Acts, and this would have been recovered from us under the insurance cover. As it was, we paid for their care and maintenance, their carriage home to England (or Wales, no doubt), and unemployment indemnity if they could not get berths on other ships.

Obviously, it would only be proper to recognize the services of the brave islanders. After consultations with the authorities, suitable sums were paid into savings banks for all of the men, and the bank books showing the credits were presented to them before a big crowd by the Governor of the territory.

About the same time, 1930 or thereabouts, I filed the papers relating to another British crew which faced a different sort of ordeal in very different surroundings, the North Atlantic ocean in winter. On that much-used route, weather is so bad so often that it is not remarkable that the International Loadline Convention insists that ships trading there in winter are loaded less deeply than anywhere else in the world. The ship in question was carrying wheat from North America to Britain. She met a real old North Atlantic gale, a bad one, bad enough to cause fractures in the steel deck plating. At the same time massive waves crashing over the bows stove in one of the forward hatches. At that time it was universal practice to close the hatchways into the holds with wooden hatch-boards and tarpaulins. The steel slab-hatches of today were unknown. Bigger ships had one or two fore and aft girders which fitted into slots in the coamings (the strong framework round the hatch opening, extending both above and below the deck) and the rows of strong boards laid athwartship were a very effective seal, when covered with three tarpaulins lashed down tight. An advantage was that casual damage could be dealt with on board. The ship carried spare boards and tarpaulins, and a ship's carpenter could even make and fit new boards if he had to.

In this case, however, the force of the waves broke some of the boards and drove them down into the hold. This of course loosened the tarpaulins, and seawater was entering both through the hatch and through the deck cracks. Enormous efforts were made by deck officers and seamen to re-cover the hatch, at the risk of being washed overboard by every wave, even though life-lines were rigged; but they had little success.

Then a worse danger appeared. As more and more water entered the hold, the wheat began to absorb the water and to swell. It pushed the remaining hatch-boards up, and even the plating of the decks. As the cracks in the plating spread, water was able to enter other holds as well. Slowly and inevitably the whole ship was bursting apart.

The captain had no alternative but to abandon the ship. An S.O.S. brought other ships, which managed to take off all the crew, despite the terrible weather. One of the rescue ships stood by until the damaged vessel sank.

Readers of C. S. Forester's *Hornblower* novels may remember how Midshipman Hornblower was left in command of a French prize, a small ship which, unknown to him, had been holed below the water-line. Her cargo of rice swelled, and she had to be abandoned. These things do happen.

Mysteries? There are many. When welding began to be used in place of riveting plates together to make merchant ships, one of the first—perhaps the first—of the all-welded ships was built at the famous Swan, Hunter shipyard on the River Tyne, and insured for crew risks with us. She was the *Joseph Medill*, a small ship destined for service in Canada on the Great Lakes, and the laws of that time did not require such a ship to carry radio. She set off on what would have been, perhaps, a fourteen-day voyage or thereabouts, and was never seen again. No wreckage, no sighting by another ship, no clue of any kind. Further ships built the same way showed no defects in the welding, and the weather was not unusual. But ship and men disappeared, and no-one knows why.

Comedy? In New Orleans, a black longshoreman employed to discharge cargo fell down the hold, a distance of thirty-two feet, landed on his head on a steel deck, got up, and walked away totally unhurt.

Comedy of the sea, however, sometimes has odd undertones. During the 1939-45 war, I had to enquire into a collision between two Dutch ships. The captain of the one which we insured, a tanker owned by Shell, came into the office to give his story of the accident. Bit by bit, my secretary took it down. A convoy of ships bound for Bristol was following a swept channel through a British minefield at night. There was only room to move safely in single file, a tricky business with dimmed and shaded lights. The Shell tanker carried the convoy commodore, and was number one, leading the line. Suddenly, the captain told me, he saw the loom of a ship in the darkness—a darker darkness, as it were—crossing his course from right to left. Before he could slow, he hit the other ship on her stern.

I asked whether the other ship was one of the convoy. Yes, he answered, she should have been in the number 8 position in the line, a mile or two astern. 'Whatever was the man doing, then?' I asked. 'Oh!' said my Dutchman casually, 'he was just taking a short cut across the mine-field to get first pilot, and then get away on shore leave.'

The first witness ever from whom I took a statement myself was a Thames river-pilot, who had been in charge of a BP tanker bound down river, when she collided with a Thames spritsail barge. Artists still love to paint these graceful, great vessels with their russet sails. They used to be a familiar sight on the Thames and the nearby coasts. A few, privately owned, can still be seen in places like Maldon, but none trades any more, and the annual barge race has, I believe, been abandoned.

As regards the collision, steam vessels have to give way to sail, but the sailing vessel has to obey certain rules. The pilot was very emphatic that these rules had been ignored. 'In fact,' he said, 'I hailed her skipper and told him so.' My secretary took down his statement in shorthand, and went off to type it out for signature. The pilot mused a little, then hitched his chair a little

B

nearer, and said, 'Now the young lady's gone, sir, I'll tell you exactly what I said to him.'

Such a stream of reports came into us at the office that one was tempted to think that sea trade was an unending pageant of accidents, violence and excitement. Of course, the opposite is the case. On most voyages nothing much happens. My wife and I were lucky enough to do a number of short trips in cargo ships, and still regard it as an ideal holiday for anyone who is not subject to sea-sickness, and who sometimes likes to do nothing at all except look at the sea and sky. If these trips were added together, they would make, I suppose, two or three months, or even four. In the whole of that time, the nearest we came to a collision was when the *Khuzistan* was at Grangemouth, and the ship astern of her, moving out of berth, scraped her stern enough to remove a little paint. The London streets are more dangerous to motorcars than the Channel is to ships. But it's true the accidents are rather bigger accidents at sea.

Besides the physical accidents, I also had to deal with a vast range of purely financial disputes. Sometimes these were fussy little nonsenses when someone had been reading the small print in a contract, and found (or thought he had found) a way to get a small advantage. Or they could be very serious disputes. One of the Niarchos companies, for example, took delivery of a new ship, and found that her normal speed was a knot less than provided in the contract. If a ship does fourteen miles to the hour instead of fifteen for the whole of her working life of twenty years or more, it adds up to a very serious loss in her trading profits. It is, however, rather difficult to calculate in money, especially in advance. But the case went to arbitration in New York, and with the help of good lawyers the ship owner recovered a million dollars in damages from the shipbuilders.

A very different sort of case involved a ship called the *Olga*, owned by the Vlasov group. She was, I think, one of the standard Liberty-type ships built in such numbers in the U.S.A. during the 1939-45 war. The other day I heard a television commentator quote someone (perhaps President Eisenhower) who opined that the war could never have been won without the versatile DC3 aircraft and the jeep. The Liberty ship must have been an even greater factor.

The *Olga* was chartered for a period to another company, with the usual clause that when she was delivered the time-charterers would pay for any oil bunkers on board at the time, at the market price prevailing at that port. She had some hundreds of tons of bunker oil on board at the time of delivery, but an argument developed as to the price. The snag was that the port in question, Civita Vecchia in Italy, was not a bunkering port. Ships took on oil bunkers at Genoa or Savona or Leghorn. If, in an emergency, oil had to be obtained at Civita Vecchia in any quantity, it had to be brought in specially in tank lorries by road, or perhaps in a small vessel by sea. The shipowners said that the price to be paid them should be the price at the nearest bunkering port, plus these special transport charges. The charterers objected.

Arbitration was called for. A London barrister was agreed on as arbitrator, and the case was heard in his chambers in the Temple. The shipowners won the case, which I cannot recall to this day without a mental chuckle. It was of course necessary to prove the facts about the local arrangements and prices for bunkers, and we brought over a witness from Italy, the ship's agent there, Gian Franco Kielland, a good friend of mine for many years. The charterers were represented by a young junior counsel who was beginning to make a considerable reputation for himself, Mr M. R. E. Kerr, now Mr Justice Kerr. Our witness gave his evidence-in-chief, and then Michael Kerr cross-examined him. He probed and pushed from every conceivable angle, without the slightest success. Kielland's method was very simple. Whatever he was asked (or so it seemed to me), he answered 'Yes', or 'No', or 'I don't know'. When counsel asks a witness something subtle, beginning 'Do you think it possible that . . .' and gets the flat answer 'I don't know', it must be terribly frustrating.

I always said our witness won that case for us. So far, I have never had to give verbal evidence myself in court. If I do have to, I shall remember his example.

To deal with so many different kinds of dispute meant also exploring many aspects of the business world. This great web of people across the world seemed never-ending. Every week one met new people, and learnt something about new subjects.

Quite a number of times I had to handle disputes over the characteristics of different ships. When a ship was time-chartered,

like the *Olga*, the contract included in the first paragraph a statement of the deadweight capacity—the weight the ship could lift
of cargo, bunkers, and so on—the speed, and the daily fuel consumption. These are always qualified by the word 'about', and
the speed and consumption are stated as 'in good weather conditions'. With honesty and goodwill on both sides, such general
propositions cause no difficulty, but a sharp boy, whether he is
(or represents) the shipowner or the charterer, can start quite an
argument. Some of my friends the shipowners were not beyond
adding half a knot to the speed, or being a bit generous about the
deadweight.

To go thoroughly into things like this meant picking the minds
of a variety of men, the shipowner's staff, naval architects and
engineers, perhaps an expert on ship management from another
shipowner's office, surveyors and others who understand about
cargo weights and measurement, and of course lawyers.

And if a shipowner now and then would over-enthuse about
his ship's capabilities, a charterer could also make unreasonable
demands. One ship, on a voyage from Vancouver to Italy, was
described as capable of about ten and a half knots. The charterer
divided the distance between ports by ten and a half, and claimed
that the resulting number of hours was the time the ship should
have taken, and he should not pay hire for any period over that.
Eventually, he did agree that the conception was wrong as, apart
from time lost through bad weather, there was the slow passage
of the Panama Canal, and a stop at Trinidad for bunkers.

Another chartering firm, new to the business of carrying cargo
in ships hired from others, fed a lot of geographical and meteorological information into a computer, and came up with some
surprising arguments. They denied the existence of bad weather
which the captains reported, and once they refused to pay for
certain days because, they said, if the captain had taken a more
southerly route he would have avoided a storm which slowed
down the ship for a number of days. This particular firm's
relationships with shipowners were so bad that they abandoned
the shipping business after a few years.

But some of these disputes were very hard to resolve. Take the
ship which did the speed described when starting on a charter
for several years. After a year or two, she had slowed down a

great deal, although the usual regular work had been done to keep the engines in good order and the hull clean. The cause of this, the shipowners claimed, was that the charterers chose to employ the ship constantly in tropical areas, which caused an abnormal growth of weed on the ship's bottom. This was another London arbitration, which I remember particularly because both parties went before the arbitrators supported by expert witnesses, naval architects familiar with ships, and with how their speed was affected by various factors. (It is hardly necessary to say that to a charterer speed is important, if he is paying by the month. A drop in speed means fewer voyages in the year).

As it happened, the other side's expert was Charles Casebourne, a consulting marine surveyor of outstanding reputation both for knowledge of his craft and for utter integrity. He was called first, and in answers to his client's counsel he explained clearly everything in favour of that side's case. Then he was cross-examined by our side's counsel, in the course of which he quite clearly stated what could be said in favour of the shipowners. His honesty was such that the whole dispute was laid out (as far as facts were concerned) flat on the table. The only thing left to discuss was the legal question of how to interpret the words of the contract, so we decided not to call our expert to give evidence at all.

There is a cynical saying amongst lawyers : 'There are liars, there are damned liars, and there are expert witnesses.' Charlie Casebourne, that massive man, with his scholarly stoop, glasses, and carefully picked phrases, proved that wrong, and he was not the only such man. In his later years, he was often used by Lloyd's and others as an arbitrator to settle technical disputes, and his decisions were accepted without quibble.

Another man my firm has used very often as an expert adviser and expert witness works in a different field. He is a biochemist. He and his team of workers have at times worked on a very wide range of subjects, from breathalyser tests to soil conservation. If you talk with him in a relaxed way, he seems to know something about every aspect of his very wide field, and he often has pronounced opinions, too. He looks pugnacious, and indeed can be, with his short stature, broad shoulders and domed brow, but if he is given a problem, he gets down to it on classic scientific principles, and will work away at endless experiments until he is satisfied.

The first really big job he did for the firm was only marginally my concern. It was handled by a colleague, but it was important enough to touch all of us. A German shipping line carrying general cargo between Europe and South America had a series of claims for damage to coffee by taint from an unpleasant odour. The sums involved ran into hundreds of thousands of pounds in all. We were suspicious about them, partly because smell is such a very subjective matter, anyway. An attractive scent to one man is a horrible stench to another. A Frenchman's idea of how coffee should smell varies from that of an American. Also, it rather seemed that claims chiefly arose when the coffee market was in a depressed state. This could mean merely that when everyone was eager to buy, they would even buy tainted coffee without protest. It could, however, mean that, when coffee was hard to sell, some merchants would detect a taint which would support a claim on their insurers or on the shipowners.

The cause of the smell which was alleged a number of times was quite simple. The ships which carried the coffee home from Brazil carried amongst their outward cargoes various chemicals, including a pungent insecticide for use on the plantations. It was often suggested, and in one case it was established, that a drum of insecticide leaked on board the ship, and coffee was carried in that space on the return voyage. The decks had of course been carefully washed. Probably in that one case, traces had remained, but when the danger was known, it was hardly likely that the same errors would recur over and over again.

Dr Reginald Milton was commissioned to investigate all aspects of the carriage of the coffee. One is tempted to say that he sniffed along the trail from the warehouses in Germany, Belgium and Holland right back to the plantations in Brazil. Here, incidentally, he had full co-operation from the Brazilian government authorities, and it was on the plantations that he established something very interesting. He examined, cut up, and analysed different parts of the bushes, and was able to establish that insecticide was present (and could even be smelt) in the coffee beans, the leaves, the stalks and even the roots of the plants. In fact, some of the growers had been using such excessive quantities of pesticide that it was they who were causing the trouble. We helped him publish his monograph on the question. I believe his findings were never challenged, and unjustified claims came to a sudden end.

Later, he did far more extensive investigation into the carriage of maize in bulk from Argentina and Brazil to Europe. For decades, a proportion of this arrived so heated as to be useless; and there had been violent controversy as to the causes, and especially as to whether shipowners should circulate air through the holds, or seal them. Milton's work strongly supported the anti-ventilation school, threw fresh light on why and how the heating came about and exposed certain abuses in the exporting countries, neither of which exercised such a strenuous quality control on maize exports as is applied in the United States. This report caused quite a storm, which may even still be continuing. Some experts tried to disprove Milton's views on the causes of heating. However, the abuses he exposed were never denied (I hope they have been remedied), and his whole report was reprinted with approval by the Italian government, Italy being the biggest importer of maize at that time.

Activities like these saved us, over the years, millions of pounds in unjustified claims. They were so valuable that we set up a committee to co-ordinate preventive work in a number of countries. More important in the long run, they represented a check to the waste of part of the world's resources during transport and storage, a material factor in the ecological problem which so much concerns us today, the problem of how to supply what millions need.

These are a few of the subjects which have concerned me, and still concern people in my kind of world. Another was medicine, so that we could intelligently consider injury claims, and understand a doctor's report. In some countries, it seems there are occasional doctors who will certify anything. One captain claimed to be so ill with a 'rare tropical disease' that he had to have a long period of treatment in special accommodation, with nurses day and night. Our own specialist said the man's only trouble was venereal disease. And in San Francisco doctors certified an injured longshoreman as being totally incapacitated for life. This made it a little odd that within a year he made a fresh claim for injury sustained whilst working on another ship.

Civil engineering is another recurring subject (when ships hit shore installations), also navigation, the properties of metals and of every kind of material that is carried by sea, and in recent years we have had to give much attention to questions of pollution.

To help us in all these explorations, firms like mine have correspondents and consultants everywhere in the world where the ships go, and even in some places where they do not. For some twenty years I took a special interest in building for my firm a network of this kind, meeting the people, assessing their capabilities, making changes where necessary. This kind of thing is the real stuff of an international business—the human contacts. Everything depends on it.

In some countries, it was best to use lawyers, in others shipowners or ship's agency businesses as our *aides* and advisers. In one, we used a bank, in another an import/export firm. In a country where we found it difficult to deal with various commercial interests with whom we were often in conflict over claims, we finally decided to entrust our affairs to the most active of our opponents! They gladly took up the battle, when required, against the other local firms, and if their own interests were involved, at least we knew each other and could deal openly with difficulties. In certain other areas, we found it best to help local men whom we trusted to found small special businesses to handle our work. Since they only operated in that field, they were not in competition with local interests, and could give us, as their principals, quite disinterested advice.

However, based as we are in London, it was in London that much of the work had to be done, and the expert assistance found. It was usually not difficult to find.

A shipowner in a small way of business complained that he was being victimized by the Customs authorities at Recife in Brazil. He said that they had seized all the tobacco and cigarettes which were on board for the crew, and had imposed a large fine. I cabled to Recife for particulars, got them, and then telephoned to Fred Efford, who was at that time a director of a British shipowning company. 'Can you tell me,' I asked, 'roughly how many cigarettes one of your ships would carry on a round voyage to South America?' 'I'll have to check with our stores department,' he answered, 'but I'll let you know.' When he came back with the figure, I said, 'What would you think if you heard that a ship arrived out there with four million cigarettes in her stores?' 'Only one answer,' was the prompt reply. 'Smuggling.' After some thought, I wrote to the small shipowner, asking if he could explain why there was such a large quantity of cigarettes on board. I had no reply, and closed my file.

Then there was the chartering contract on which the charterers defaulted. It would have kept four or five ships busy for two years. Because of this and other losses, the shipowners concerned went into liquidation. The liquidators wanted to claim damages from the charterers for the default, and turned to me for help. In the ordinary way, the damages are calculated by comparing what the ships should have earned with what they did earn in their alternative employment. In this case, that could not be done. The fleet had been dispersed due to the liquidation, and their actual earnings were not known.

I got hold of an experienced chartering broker on London's Baltic Exchange, and he produced what was in effect a dummy schedule of earnings for the ships, based on what other ships earned during those two years. You have to know a lot about cargo movements and the variations in freight rates to do that, but on the Baltic there were dozens of men who were capable of doing it.

If a ship was sunk, and indeed in various other circumstances, it might be necessary to find its value in the free market at a certain date. Ships change ownership from country to country, and values fluctuate greatly according to supply and demand. Several of my friends, who specialize in the sale and purchase of ships as brokers in London, will give you the value of any ship at any date, past or present, within small limits. They will even estimate the cost of an imaginary ship, if you need that.

Bankers will, if approached in the right way (and by a customer!), explain the workings of foreign exchange, the borrowing of money, and the costs involved in all sorts of monetary transactions. They speak in general terms, of course. A banker is as chary of giving details of his customers' affairs as a doctor is of speaking of his patients.

Lawyers are the people we most frequently consult. They advise us on the law, but are also very good at ferreting out facts.

In London, about a score of firms of solicitors—some very large
—specialize in commercial and maritime work, and I have had
dealings with most of them in my time. I have written elsewhere
at some length about the law. There are more tales to tell, but
they can keep for another chapter.

3

The Big Money

A major marine casualty may involve the loss of one or more ships, the loss of their cargoes, damage to other property, loss of life and personal injury. This can mean major claims on three different groups of insurers.

In the same way, aviation insurers wake up in the night after dreaming about two jumbo jets colliding over the centre of New York city. Apart from the horror of the human aspects, there is the risk of massive financial loss, first of the aircraft themselves, then from the airlines' liability to their passengers in each case, and then from the public liability for people and property on whom the wreckage may fall.

In shipping casualties, we sometimes found our share—the third-party liabilities—very mixed up with that of the insurers of the ship or ships, and that of the insurers of the cargo. Sometimes, we could make common cause with them. Sometimes, it was all against all. For example, if a ship goes ashore, and she can be floated and brought in to port at a cost less than her salved value, this counts as salvage, and is paid for by insurers of the ship (and perhaps the cargo). If, however, the operation would cost too much to be worthwhile, the ship's underwriters may abandon the ship, so far as they are concerned. Then, if the wreck is in an area from which the local authorities can order it to be removed, the cost becomes an ordinary shipowner's liability, which comes under the protecting and indemnity cover, and a firm like mine is in the centre of the picture.

As well as this basic question of insurances which may run alongside or else against each other, there is the great web of reinsurance, by which all major marine insurers spread the effects of the bigger accidents. If, therefore, a big one happens, there is a good chance that every marine insurer in many countries will be involved, more or less.

What are the big ones, and how big are they? I look at them, of course, from the shipowners' liability angle. Our records show that year by year somewhere about half the total we paid out was for personnel claims (injury, illness and death, seamen, stevedores, passengers and others) and another quarter cargo claims (when the shipowners had to pay for loss or damage to cargo). But much of this was made up by thousands and thousands of small or moderate claims.

The big ones nowadays (except for a few big cargo claims) tend to fall into other classes. One is pollution, a subject which merits, I think, a chapter to itself. The other two are wreck removal, and explosion and fire. These are the types of claim which were most likely to run into several millions of pounds.

For centuries, fire has been the most feared hazard for the seaman. This may seem odd when there is so much water about to put out a fire, but the peril consists in the confinement of a group of people in a small space, and the distance of perhaps hundreds of miles between them and any outside help. Add to this the facts that for most of human history ships have been built of highly combustible material, and that many cargoes burn easily and fiercely.

The great Atlantic liner *United States*, probably the finest civilian product of American shipbuilding, was designed to minimize the fire hazard. When she was new, I was shown over her at Southampton by United States Lines' U.K. operations manager Ted Cook. He told me that the only wood in the ship was in the grand pianos and in the butchers' chopping blocks. But it must be remembered that in her tanks there were thousands of tons of oil, so that even with all the expensive substitutions used (above the main deck everything was aluminium to give also lightness and strength) the bogey of the fire risk could not be wholly exorcized.

Many of us can remember the reports and the pictures of fires in passenger ships, *L'Atlantique* in the Channel, the Greek Line's *Lakonia* in the North Atlantic, the *Normandie* (fortunately empty of passengers) alongside her New York berth, and back in the nineteen thirties the *Morro Castle*, which carried so many gay crowds in luxury between New York and Havana. Not all these tragedies, some of which caused heavy loss of life, involved my firm. We had a reinsurance line (a small percentage) on the *Morro Castle*. We paid out nearly a million pounds for the *Lakonia*.

The biggest of all, however, did not concern crowded and expensive passenger liners, but the workhorses of the sea, the run-of-the-mill cargo ships which had been produced by the hundred during the Second World War. The place was Texas City. The ships occupying the central roles were three in number, one French (the *Grandcamp*) and two American, one of which had an ironical name in the circumstances—the *Highflier*. All were loading similar cargoes of fertilizer, a type much used then, mostly consisting of ammonium nitrate. It was not realized by most of the people involved, if indeed by any of them, that this variety could not merely catch fire, but could also cause explosions. And that is what happened. A fire was followed by a series of explosions which destroyed the three ships, damaged many more, and flattened a large part of the town. Hundreds were killed; perhaps no one ever knew the exact number. Likewise, no one ever knew the exact total of the material damage. The legal and insurance issues which developed became impossibly tangled, and although we had a share in the insurances on the American ships, I never found out quite what was the final result. Certainly, the U.S. government itself had to intervene, and take much of the burden off those who suffered. The total sums involved were hundreds of millions of dollars.

We had been asked a little while before to quote premiums to insure the liabilities of the French ship. The owners thought our premiums too high, and refused our terms, to our good fortune.

A very short time after the Texas City explosion, the *Ocean Liberty*, carrying the same type of fertilizer, blew up off the French port of Brest.

During the Second World War a serious explosion occurred in Bombay in the *Fort Stikine*, discharging general cargo. As I recall, it is thought to have had its origin in a fire in bales of raw cotton in the ship's hold, possibly by some negligent person dropping a lighted cigarette; but there were explosives on board also, and when the ship blew up, the whole island of Bombay felt the shock.

It was estimated that five hundred people were killed and a thousand seriously injured. Ten ships were lost, or so damaged as to be past repair; and the area of almost total devastation was about a mile across. When I was in India in 1964, over twenty years later, I was told how gold ingots from the ship's strong-room fell from the sky into the garden of a house on Cullaba Hill, literally miles away from the docks. This shocking accident occurred, however, at a crucial stage in the war. In the confused conditions, normal safety precautions were largely disregarded. For example, most major ports only allow explosives to be loaded or discharged at a special berth, far away from inhabited areas; and, partly for this reason, explosives are usually handled on a 'last in, first out' basis. International rules for the carriage of hazardous cargo have been tightened in recent years. Such an accident as the Bombay explosion is far less likely today.

A case I dealt with myself was the Greek ship *Nicolas Epiphaniades*, which blew up in Odessa harbour when loading a part cargo of coal, with some vehicles, for Asian ports. Much damage was done to port sheds, and the ship was effectively a total loss. A bull-dozer stowed on deck was never seen again. It was presumed that it landed in deep water somewhere in the port area.

A curious feature was that two official enquiries were held, one by the Greek government and one by the Russian government. The Greek enquiry attached no blame to the ship. It seemed to me perfunctory and possibly biased, but it may simply have been that they could not get the evidence of the shore witnesses. The Russian report was very detailed and painstaking. It seemed that the coal came from a mine in the Don basin, which was known to supply coal of a very 'gassy' nature. Gas and dust from the loading had evidently collected in one of the underdeck spaces, forming an explosive mixture. There were several possible causes for the ignition. An electric spark was one. But the report included a description by a woman doctor of injuries to two of the crew. One of them had extensive burns on his face, hands and forearms. Had this happened as he lit a cigarette in that gas-filled space?

Human casualties were relatively light. No one, as I recall now, was killed. The Russians started legal proceedings in Odessa and threatened to do so in Greece; but a settlement was reached, one condition of which was that they kept what was left of the ship in part settlement of the damages.

Sometimes, the end result of an accident of this kind can be quite different in insurance terms from what one might expect. Such was the case with the French ship *La Coubre*. Not long after the Castro revolution, she was discharging in Havana a mixed cargo, including explosives, when she blew up. The first estimate of the damage done to the city was eight million pounds. The ship's liabilities were not insured with us, but by good friends of ours. Their top man got on the first practicable flight to investigate on the spot. Before he arrived, however, President Castro had made an immediate investigation, and announced on the national radio that the cause of the explosion was sabotage by counter-revolutionaries. Fortunately for the insurers, there was no later attempt to show that the losses were due to any cause for which the shipowners were responsible, so there was no claim.

In the years immediately before my retirement, the biggest claims in our office were for wreck removal. Three occur to me at once, the *Tritonica*, the *Wahine*, and the *Seawise University*, all of which were handled by other partners in the firm. Before dealing with them I should like to set the stage, as it were, by telling the story of another lesser claim which I dealt with myself.

The *Mitera Marigo* was a ship built in Yugoslavia for one of the several Lemos firms, which all originate from the same family or group of families of that name from the small island of Oinoussoi, off Chios in Greece. The firm was controlled by George Christos Lemos and his brother Michael. She collided in the Channel with a German vessel, one of the Thyssen ships, and was badly damaged forward. Number 1 hold was flooded. At a slow speed, she managed to reach Falmouth without tug assistance, but it was a near thing. If the weather had worsened, she might not have made it.

She was carrying a cargo of iron ore, a fact which had a great bearing on what followed. One tends to think of ore as a romantic mineral, but iron ore is of course simply rock and dust, containing iron in various chemical combinations. It is cheap, and very heavy, so heavy that an ordinary cargo ship, when fully laden with iron ore, contains only a flattish, cone-shaped heap of ore at the bottom of each hold. If she is a ship with 'tween-decks, a proportion may be shot into the 'tween-decks (ore is usually loaded from chutes) to give a better weight distribution.

The pilot who boarded the damaged *Mitera Marigo* as she entered Falmouth consulted with the harbour-master, who ordered her to anchor at the deep-water mooring in the harbour, at a bend of the River Fal. So far, so good. But next morning there was a bang like an explosion, and cracks appeared in the deck forward. The ship began to sink by the head. The crew scrambled for the boats, and got clear in time to see their ship disappear (but for the masts) below the surface.

I had been informed of the collision and helped to arrange the legal investigation as to which ship was to blame, a matter which itself produced a good deal of work over the next two or three years, and a lawsuit.

However, the next aspect of the case to hit me was not the removal of wreck question, but a different one. George Lemos appeared in my office, together with H. J. Scott, marine claims manager of Hobbs, Savill & Co., brokers who had placed the insurances on the ship's hull, machinery and freight, spread over Lloyd's underwriters and various insurance companies. A claim had been made against the insurer for over a million pounds, and they were refusing to pay, on the grounds that they were not satisfied that the ship was a total loss. George Lemos wanted me to help him in starting a legal action to recover the money right away, that very day, if possible.

The Greeks are not trained to keep a stiff upper lip in times of stress. If they feel strongly about something, they tend to let you know, very forcibly, and often their feelings are made apparent to everyone within a wide radius. Michael P., a well-known shipowner in London, once said to one of my partners, 'I like to lunch at the Greek restaurant in the City, because I can shout there.'

George Lemos was, shall we say, a trifle emphatic. I explained to him that the ship was in a sheltered harbour, and the underwriters could with reason ask for time to have an underwater inspection, and to consider their position before paying out such a sum. I agreed, however, to arrange such an inspection ourselves, so that we would know the exact facts, too.

It seemed to me that the pair were back before my desk every day for the next month. The theme was always 'Why can't I have my money now?' No doubt it is very upsetting to lose a good profit-earning ship when you still have to pay off most of the value in instalments, for she was only built the year before. It may well have been, too, that the Lemos Bros. business needed a million pounds odd of available cash just then. 'Scottie' strongly supported me in persuading the irate shipowner to hold his hand, and after about a month the claim was admitted and paid. I may say in passing that H.J.S., now retired, was in my opinion unsurpassed as a marine claims man. He not only had an immense knowledge of the subject, but he also understood intimately the men who held the purse strings, their feelings and way of thinking. He knew when to wait, when to press vigorously, and when to wheedle. And he was a friend to all.

Half way through the month, we got the report of the divers, who told an unhappy story. The bang which signalled the start of the trouble had not, apparently, been the deck cracking but the transverse steel bulkhead between numbers one and two holds, welded to the side plating of the ship on each side, breaking clean away. Since the ore cargo was only a few feet high at the bottom of the hold, it offered no resistance to the thousands of tons of water in number one, pressing against the forward side of the bulkhead, and the pressure had proved too much. The shock, combined with the weakening of shell and deck by the collision damage, caused the deck to fracture right across. Water rushed aft into the next hold, and the enormous strain as the fore part of the ship bent downwards had caused another series of fractures further aft. The ship had virtually broken into three pieces. Moreover, the sudden inrush of water had made her dive nose first to the bottom with an impact which drove the ship's forefoot thirty-two feet deep into the mud of the River Fal.

All the experts considered it impossible to lift the ship in one piece, which of course did not add to our pleasure when the harbour commissioners served a notice calling upon the shipowners to remove the wreck. I instructed the solicitor we had engaged on the shipowners' behalf (that same Reggie Parkin I described in Chapter 1) to decline. The commissioners informed us that they would do it at their own expense, and would recover

c

the cost from the shipowners in due course, if necessary by legal means.

They contracted for the work to be done and kept us advised of progress. The method used was to cut up the ship into small pieces (underwater cutting of metal is no novelty nowadays, any more than welding is on land), and take it ashore bit by bit. First came the masts, funnel and superstructure, then the ship's hull down to the level of the tank tops (the top of the double bottom). Even the propeller and shafting were removed. Finally, the cargo of iron ore was spread as smoothly as possible over the area, to make it a safe mooring ground for the future.

Meanwhile, we were going deeply into the legal position, for I was determined not to pay this claim, unless legally compelled to do so. Three lines of defence were set up. The first was that the Falmouth Harbour Authority ought not to be indemnified for losses arising out of their own fault. It was they who decided the ship should moor at the deep-water berth. They knew she was damaged; and, if they had allocated her to as shallow a berth as possible, she would have settled gently on the mud, and could have been repaired and lifted without difficulty.

The second argument was that the cost of removing the wreck was so excessive (some £160,000) that it was quite unjustifiable, just to clear one of the port's several moorings. The third was the perhaps rather subtle one that the shipowners did not own the cargo of iron ore, and that it was impracticable to consider removing the ship until the ore had been removed by whoever was deemed responsible for that.

All these things depended to a large extent on the special act of parliament defining the powers of the harbour authority. This provided that the owner of any property which became an obstruction to navigation in the harbour could be called upon to remove it. If he failed to do so, the authority could do the work, and recover the reasonable cost of it from the owner of the property. Eventually, I consulted no less than three Queen's Counsel on these points, and none of them would support my arguments. For example, on the issue of reasonableness, they considered that the cost had to be reasonable for the work to be done, and that it was not open to us to argue that it was unreasonable to do the work. The cost was the equivalent of the entire income of the port for a number of years; but I understood privately that the government had insisted on the berth being cleared, for reasons connected with defence. It was the only sheltered deep-water berth in the bay, and in both world wars it had been much used by damaged ships seeking refuge, and by naval vessels.

I had been battling along on these lines for two or three years, before I was finally convinced by our own lawyers that it would be useless to take the matter to court. Meanwhile, the harbour commissioners and their lawyers asked us to attend a conference with them and their insurers, on the basis that if a settlement could not be reached, a writ would be issued. We agreed to attend.

The shipowners said they would leave it to us. It was our money at stake. So the day came when I set off with Reggie Parkin down Lime Street, alongside Lloyd's, to the meeting. As we strolled along, I said to him, 'Whatever are we going to say to these fellows?' 'I don't know,' he replied, 'there's nothing much we can say.' We agreed that I should be spokesman.

The room seemed crammed with them, a couple of Cornishmen from the port authority, a whole group of underwriters, amongst whom I recognized the late 'Toby' Green, probably the most enterprising and unconventional man at Lloyd's at that time, and in the centre their solicitor Donald O'May, an old adversary. He very often acted (and acts) against shipowners, but at other times for them, as is quite the custom in the City. He was about to launch into an introductory speech, which I expected to be long and caustic, when I anticipated him by saying: 'Donald, I think we can cut this meeting short. We have decided we will have to pay.' The line of faces looked amusingly blank for a moment, then Toby Green hooted with laughter, and everybody (I think) smiled. I added, 'The only question is, really, how much we pay. We could argue the whole claim with you, item by item, but it would be better, perhaps, to leave it to you to let us off as lightly as you reasonably can.' There did not seem much more which could sensibly be said, so Reggie and I made our good-byes and went.

Outside, in Lime Street, he looked at me and laughed. As far as I recall, he heard from O'May a week or so later that his clients would accept a little over £150,000, plus a few thousand pounds in costs. This probably represented a modest saving.

Looking back on the case, I wonder. Was I making a heroic defence against overwhelming odds, or was I merely being stubborn, flogging my own point of view against good sense and good advice as well as against the opposition? I fear that it was more likely stubbornness. I wanted to believe that the law would support my view, and therefore kept telling myself that what I thought the logical view would be that of the law, too.

I do not subscribe to Mr Bumble's view that 'the law is a ass', but English law, at any rate, is not a cold, logical, comprehensive code. As most of us know, it springs from various sources, Roman, Anglo-Saxon, Norman-French and many others. I recommend, for a view of one stage of its development, Sir Arthur Bryant's account of King Henry II—in *Makers of the Realm*, I think. Henry did much to preserve the best of the Anglo-Saxon heritage of precedents and trial by jury and to fit it together with the best features of the feudal system.

For the last fifty years or more, the work of past centuries has been enriched by international viewpoints, as conventions and agreements, especially those of the League of Nations and the United Nations Organization, have been incorporated by Westminster into English law.

The net result is of course a compromise, but a rich, flexible and generally effective fabric of laws. It is not surprising if at some points it departs from my point of view, or the next man's, but we can all be deeply grateful for it as a whole. Life in a complex society would be impossible without it.

The other three wrecks which cost us heavily were all different in cause, type and location. None of them was dealt with by me personally, but I often talked them over in the office with the people who did so.

One was the *Tritonica*, an ore carrier on her way, fully laden, from Seven Islands to a steel-works deep in the Great Lakes. Below Montreal she collided with another ship and sank. The wreck, pinned down by her cargo of iron ore, blocked half of the navigable channel of the St Lawrence river, and the Canadian government were naturally insistent that the wreck be promptly cleared. The task was a difficult one, for there was a six-knot current in the river. Local salvors found it impossible to lift the wreck, and decided to cut it down, in the same manner as was used for the *Mitera Marigo*. For this purpose, they anchored over the wreck a big barge carrying a heavy derrick. Even with the upper works cut away, the ship was still an obstruction, so the barge was shifted downstream a little. There, with huge grabs, the salvors dug a deep channel alongside, into which (with the help of the current) the wreck eventually fell, until it was below the level of the river-bed. A costly business.

The second was the *Wahine*, the big ferry of the Union Steam Ship Company of New Zealand, which connected the north and south islands of New Zealand. Bound inwards for Wellington, her captain received a storm warning, and decided that the safest course was to stand on for harbour. My colleague who flew out after the accident was told that two weather fronts apparently met over the ship as she reached the entrance, that the wind was gusting up to 120 miles an hour, and shifting direction up to 180 degrees. The air must have been full of water, and visibility by eye or radar down to nil. In those conditions, it was hardly surprising that the ship hit the rocks.

The most astonishing thing to me was the relatively small loss of life : 51, I believe it was, out of the hundreds on board. Some passengers, young and old, were blown bodily through the water some seven miles on to the beach on the other side of the harbour, and lived.

Under our insurances we had of course to pay for the life and injury claims, but the biggest money cost to us was for removal of wreck. It was hoped for some time that it would be possible to float this seven-decked ship by filling her spaces with expanded plastic—rather like filling her with table-tennis balls—and then tow her round the coast and sink her in deep water. However, further storms the next winter so damaged her bottom and side, that she was clearly unfloatable. It was a question of cutting her up on the spot, and taking her away in small pieces. There were several thousand tons of steel in the ship, and in those rough waters it was a mammoth job. We paid the salvors on a 'cost plus' basis, as a fixed price contract was impracticable, and payments were made every month or two. I remember our passing the two million pound mark, and the three million mark, and I think the four, but I don't know the final figure, as the job was still unfinished when I retired in 1972.

The third case was also still going strong when I retired, and resulted from a disaster which made news headlines all over the world. The *Seawise University* had been the Cunarder *Queen Elizabeth*, built in 1940, 83,000 gross tons, 1,031 feet long, and for over 20 years the biggest ship in the world. When she became no longer economic for passenger service, she was bought by Mr C. Y. Tung, a leading Hong Kong shipowner, for conversion into a floating university at Hong Kong. He spent millions of pounds on the conversion.

One of my partners was actually in Hong Kong, invited to attend the gala dinner for the opening of the new university, when he heard that the ship was on fire, and the fire out of control. He saw Mr Tung a day or two later. We Westerns think of the Chinese (quite wrongly, I suspect) as an impassive race. My partner told me that Mr Tung could not speak of the affair without his eyes filling with tears. In a matter of hours his dream had ended, his great project for the good of the colony frustrated.

The pictures after the fire were among the saddest I have seen of any material object. The 'Queen' (she and her sister *Queen Mary* had for long been 'the Queens' to millions) had been one of the most beautiful ships afloat. Now she lay tilted on the mud, her funnels askew, the graceful bridge and upper works distorted and even part melted by the fierce flames, the lovely curves of her hull transformed overnight into a clumsy, rusting hulk. The thousand tons and more of oil in her fuel tanks were an imminent danger to the entire harbour, and she was perched on the edge of the channel leading to Hong Kong's new berths for container ships.

I cannot tell everything about the removal of wreck claim, partly for business reasons, partly because I do not know everything, and partly because the story is still not ended. As recently as December 1975, the wreck was reported as shifting, and taking a further list. However, the sums involved again ran into millions of pounds, more than with the *Wahine*. There was, too, a further complication.

An official enquiry was held into the cause of the fire, presided over by a distinguished London lawyer brought over for the purpose. This disclosed that there had been many small fires during the long process of converting the ship for use as a university. This is not remarkable. Such fires are fairly common during any major reconstruction of a ship, because large quantities of combustible material are scattered about, hundreds of workers unfamiliar with shipboard risks are working all over the place, and the usual routines, including normal safety inspections and fire drills, are necessarily suspended. These conditions explain why so many major ship fires happen when the ship is in a shipyard. In normal good conditions (and in the case of the *Seawise University*) special firefighting squads are constantly on duty, and they deal at once with these casual small fires.

The enquiry, however, came to the conclusion that the major fire was the result of a number of simultaneous outbreaks and, whilst not making a definite finding, stated that the most likely cause was sabotage. Just why a project like this should be sabotaged is quite a mystery, but so much of the violence of recent years seems utterly purposeless to most people, and justified only by thoroughly twisted reasoning.

The result of the enquiry produced a very grave insurance problem. Sabotage is, in marine insurance, included in cover against war risks, which are insured (as a rule) separately from the ordinary sea perils. Different policies covered the ship herself against war and marine perils. The same applied to the liabilities, including liability for removal of wreck. The underwriters were different and even the insured value—the limit on what could be paid. It seemed for a time that the difference of interest between the shipowners and the various insurers would produce deadlock and result in a difficult lawsuit. It says a good deal for the London insurance market that eventually this aspect was resolved by amicable agreement.

Quite a few accidents of this kind came to my notice at different times, and some had strange and bizarre aspects. There was the Belgian steamer *Brabo*, which foundered off the River Tyne during the Second World War, and had to be removed from the middle of a minefield. There was the barge full of drums of chlorine which sank off New Orleans and threatened to contaminate the city's water supply. And there was a ship which sank near the coast of Venezuela. The only way to remove her was by blasting. It would be necessary to reduce her to fragments small enough not to be a menace to ships navigating or anchoring in the area. The local people seemed nervous of it, and my partner Sidney

Fowler decided to ask our New York correspondents if they could find and send an expert to superintend the work. They replied by cable, 'Propose to send our director Norman De Weir whose sea service included three years with salvage company with extensive blasting experience.' Sidney regrettably replied, 'Approve De Weir. We had no idea he was so blasted good.'

However, since personnel claims still provide in the aggregate the biggest element in liability insurance, this chapter on 'the big money' must cover them also. They were never a speciality of mine, although I handled a lot of such claims for a few wartime years, and occasional ones during most of my working life.

I never liked that side of the business. Occasionally, the facts were sickening, but we rarely came in direct contact with the people concerned, the sick or injured or the dependants of those who died. Nearly everything came to us at a second or third remove, and it was so repetitive in character that one's sensibilities were blunted. The issues involved were few in number, and the claims were so many, that it was shamefully easy to lapse into a routine. In fact, my firm, like most others, uses specialists to deal with most of these claims. I hope they are better than I ever was at seeing each claim in human terms; and I think they are.

The great bulk of our claims arise in Britain and the United States. In many countries, life and limb are still held cheap; and in many others there are such comprehensive state welfare schemes for the sick and injured, and for the bereaved, that claims against employers do not arise, or are not encouraged by law. Yugoslavia, for some twenty years after it was established as a Communist state, did not allow claims against employers. Then it was decided that a worker could sue his employer for damages, if the employer was at fault, in addition to claiming the state welfare benefits. The situation is therefore much the same there as in Britain in this respect.

In the U.S.A., longshoremen and stevedores get compensation from their employers if injured at work, regardless of the cause of the injury, but others, including seamen, are not so privileged. Anyone, however, can sue his employer for damages for negligence, as can anyone in Britain, too. Over the years, the courts have put heavy duties on employers in both countries as regards liability for injuries at work.

In England in the nineteenth century, Parliament by the Factory Acts was already making rules about safety in working places. An employer who broke the rules got fined, and also had to pay damages if a man was hurt.

But the common law of England goes much further than that. In London, not many years back, a ship was loading general cargo. Cases of different goods were stacked at one end of the hold. They were not very evenly stowed, and the gang of men working together thought they would try to even them out. The next sling-load which came down was a big roll of newsprint paper, weighing maybe a ton and a half. They started swinging it, as it hung in air, and banging it against the stock of cargo. Unexpectedly, it spun round, and a man was crushed against the cargo. The employer was found liable for his injuries, on the ground of failing to provide a safe system of working. The fact that the injured man was himself judged to be negligent operated only to reduce the award.

In America, one common ground for an action by a seaman or shore worker is a failure to provide a seaworthy ship. Of course, there have been many cases where something was truly wrong, a worn rope, a rusted ladder, and even sometimes a whole ship which had somehow slipped through her periodical examination for seaworthiness without proper upkeep. But the obligation to provide a ship 'seaworthy' for a man to work on has been carried sometimes to rather extreme lengths by American judges and juries. It may be just a patch of oil on the deck under a winch, which is alleged to be 'unseaworthiness'. When the States Steamship Company's *Iowa* was lost in a storm on the bar of the Columbia River in Oregon, one of the allegations of unfitness was the lack of telephone communication between the bows and the bridge. In those days, no ordinary cargo ship had such equipment. A Greek seaman, ashore on leave with shipmates ten miles or more from another ship, was stabbed by a fellow-seaman. A United States judge and jury held that the ship was unseaworthy, because the shipowner employed a man prone to violence among the crew.

The case, however, which produced most hollow laughter in the office, when we read the report of it in *American Maritime Cases*, was in a court in Texas, and concerned a man injured in an attack by a German submarine. His ship was held to be un-seaworthy because she carried no gun to fight off submarines.

A great number of injury suits in the U.S.A. go for jury trial. The juries, no doubt, feel that it is usually the case of a little man against a big shipowner who is backed by a wealthy insurance company. I once dealt with the case of the young chief officer of an American flag ship who was washed overboard and drowned. The accident occurred in a violent gale in the North Atlantic. Damage had been done by the waves to the ship, and to avoid the wreckage doing further damage it was essential to lash up what had come adrift. The captain brought the ship head to wind and sea, and reduced speed to mere steerage way. Lifelines were rigged, and the chief officer, boatswain and a couple of seamen set to work. Every precaution was taken, but mountainous waves broke one of the lifelines, and the man disappeared.

The case was handled for us by an eminent firm of lawyers who have acted for my firm for perhaps 80 or 100 years. They are, in the opinion of many, the most prominent in maritime affairs, conservative and painstaking, even though, when I last visited New York, they had just installed a large computer in their office on Broadway to assist in information retrieval, as well as money matters. Their clients include many famous names. On this occasion they sent me a detailed legal opinion on the case, reviewing the evidence, and ending something to this effect : 'You will therefore see that no evidence of any kind has been produced which indicates a possibility of fault on the part of the shipowner. We cannot imagine any basis on which the action can succeed. On the other hand, the widow is young and very attractive, and we cannot recommend that you expose her to a susceptible New York jury. We therefore advise that you authorize us to settle the claim on the best possible terms.'

It is perhaps not surprising that, in such a huge, free-wheeling society as the United States of America, abuses arise in this area of the law. For a number of years, some time back now, it seemed to us that one particular lawyer virtually had a monopoly in prosecuting seamen's injury claims against shipowners in New York. When I was a filing clerk, one of our files contained two newspaper cuttings about this lawyer, admittedly in the later stages of his career. One reported divorce proceedings by his wife who cited 200 co-respondents. The other reported evidence put forward in support of a demand that he be disbarred, alleging that he took for his fee one half of any sum a plaintiff recovered in an injury suit. He maintained a boarding-house in the suburbs where his clients could live whilst awaiting a hearing of their claims, perhaps for a year or two years. The charges made for this altruistic service were also, it was said, deducted from the award. He was in fact barred from practice, but some years later I read a report that he had been reinstated.

Some of that country's local papers have been known to publish articles on lawyers who have left the locality to practise law in a big city, listing the awards obtained from juries for personal injury claimants, almost as though they were baseball results or athletic records. (A big verdict gets the headlines in England, too.) One very successful lawyer of this type wrote a book on how to get big verdicts from juries. It was summarized in *Life*, or one of the other big illustrated papers of the time. One point he made was to this effect: 'When you call a doctor as a witness, don't ask him what treatment he gave your client. Hold up a surgical saw in sight of the jury, and ask him what kind of noise it makes as it goes through the bone.'

On one occasion he represented a woman who had lost a leg in a train accident. On the first day of the trial, he carried into court a large object, some two feet six inches or three feet long, approximately round in section, thick at one end and tapering towards the other, with a projection at the narrow end, sticking out at right angles. This was swathed in butcher's muslin. He placed it very carefully in the most conspicuous position on his desk. At the end of the day, he picked it up and carried it carefully out. The same procedure was followed each day until his final address to the jury began. At one point in this he stopped, paused for a long moment, then slowly unwrapped the package, in complete silence. One or two of the jurors went white. Inside was an artificial leg. Holding this up, he said to the jury: 'How would you like to wear this for the rest of your life?' He told this story himself in his book.

There are 'ambulance-chasers' in Britain, too, I fear, though they are not as flamboyant as some of those across the Atlantic. I suppose those lawyers who prosecute the claims of injured people span the whole ethical range from selfless care for those who suffer to a wholly cynical money-making based on the same suffering. Their opponents are mostly, in effect, insurance companies. It is hard for these companies to be fair, humane, or compassionate. The most I can claim is that most of us try to do this, as far as we can, and we sometimes succeed.

Perhaps my dissatisfaction with personal injury work may be linked with the impossibility of assessing human suffering in terms of money. How much is a broken leg worth? What is the value of a human life?

Not long ago, two accidents in England caused heavy loss of life, the London Underground train crash at Moorgate Station, and the fire at the Summerland amusement centre in the Isle of Man. Children were among those killed, and some parents expressed violent indignation at being offered compensation of £250 or £500 for a lost child.

Their natural feelings were due to a misconception. The law of damages does not attempt to assess the value of a life, but only the financial loss resulting to other people (particularly to dependants) from the death. When a child is killed, the parents suffer financially for immediate expenses, but they rarely suffer a loss of income. In terms of money, they may well be better off in the following years. So also with the older people. If I were to be killed now, my children could not show they were worse off by my death for they are fully independent.

For this reason, in the case of a disaster where a number of people are killed, insurers expect that a proportion of the claims will produce nominal liability, or none. Premiums are assessed in this expectation. But many of the uninitiated think of employers' liabilities, airlines' liabilities, shipowners' liabilities, in the same context as life insurance or accident insurance. But life and accident insurances are simply a guarantee that if a particular event occurs, an agreed sum of money shall be paid, unconditionally.

In liability insurance, the big money awards for personal accidents are for loss of earnings of a highly paid person, or for expensive medical treatment which will continue for a long period.

There is another very common misconception over this whole business—the idea that 'the insurance will pay', and the cost is therefore immaterial. People imagine a vast pool of money from which the injured may draw to any extent without affecting anything but themselves and this great anonymous spring of wealth. The idea is totally bogus. The cost of insurance is at once put on to the cost of living generally. Loss or damage to goods in transit, damage to the ships, trucks, trains and aircraft which carry them, injuries to people who are involved in the transit, all go into the ultimate price of the goods to the consumer. The same applies to most other forms of insurance. When all the accounts are settled, 'the big money' comes out of your pockets and mine. Insurers therefore always feel conscious of the limits which must be put on their payments of claims. They cannot and should not be over-generous.

These points need to be weighed by people who seek to extend liabilities further. For example, a few countries already provide absolute liability on the road. If your motor car hits and injures someone, you pay, even if it is entirely the other fellow's fault. It has even been argued that the overall cost of this system is less than one based on blame and negligence, owing to the saving in legal costs. It is true, I believe, that in civil matters, as distinct from criminal, the British courts are clogged with cases of two particular kinds, matrimonial disputes and 'running-down cases' (road accidents). And this is despite the fact that third-party insurance is compulsory by law for all users of motor vehicles, so that almost all running-down cases involve insurers.

Muddy thinkers, sentimentalists, vote-catching politicians are all prone to promote new liabilities on a 'Why should they suffer?' basis. But we all need to consider what things should fall on the community as a whole, and what should be borne by the individual.

Perhaps I may end this chapter by recalling a bad accident which my firm dealt with, but for which we paid nothing. The reason was simple. It was none of our business, although we made it our concern.

Just after I arrived at work one day a caller was announced to me, Mr Alan Reardon Smith from Cardiff, a director of Sir William Reardon Smith & Sons, Ltd. He was ill at ease, and obviously a worried man. He said something to this effect: 'If you have seen the newspapers, you can guess what I have come about'. I nodded. 'We have this new ship, the *Queen City*, just completed in an English shipyard. We were flying in a crew from India, and yesterday the chartered aircraft crashed at Mont Blanc in France, and all were killed. My insurers will not help, and I don't know what to do.'

The situation was certainly unusual. The Reardon Smith Line was one of a number of British shipowning companies which had (and still have) a long tradition of employing seamen from India and Pakistan in their vessels. Agreements on these matters have existed for decades with the governments concerned, and with the local and the British seamen's unions. The earnings of these men are important for their countries and for their families and villages. An officer of the Strick Line once described to me how they paid off the entire crew in Marmagoa, then the chief port in Portuguese Goa, after a year and a half of service abroad. The whole crowd cycled off on brand-new bicycles for their home villages in nearby Maharashtra State. Each carried a crate of crockery or other household equipment bought abroad. A few hours later, they were all back alongside, and the officer had to sign Customs documents for them all to get the bicycles and other goods across the Indian border.

On board another ship the steward said to me proudly: 'I come from a P. and O. village.' In this remote Indian village the principal employer for generations had been the great Peninsular & Oriental Steamship Company, far away in London.

Now forty-four of these seamen's crushed bodies lay in the snow, high in the French Alps.

Reardon Smith spread the P. and I. insurance for their considerable fleet between our 'club' and two others. The *Queen City* had been entered in advance with one of our rivals, but that club took the view (justifiably) that the insurance had not begun, and consequently they declined to act. Some of the forty-four men were Indian, some Pakistani. All had been signed on ship's articles before the Shipping Master in Calcutta, and therefore were already members of the crew.

'I know nothing about aviation law,' said Alan Reardon Smith. Nor did I; nor did my younger colleague Sidney Fowler, who was also present, but we had been trained to regard it as our primary task to help our shipowner members. I therefore said : 'Leave it all to us.'

We found out who were the solicitors most experienced in aviation law; and their help was invaluable. Sidney did most of the work. I merely sat in on some of the conferences. We found that the probable cause of the accident was that the aircraft, chartered by Reardon Smith from Air India International, was fifty miles off its expected course; but this was never proved. In any event the airline was responsible in the circumstances.

The bigger job, one of niggling detail, was to seek out the dependants of the forty-four men in their homes and find out their entitlement under their respective Workmen's Compensation Acts. In this we were greatly helped by our solicitors in Bombay for the Indians; and for the Pakistanis by the Commercial Counsellor to the High Commissioner for Pakistan in London. By these means, financial relief was able to reach the bereaved families six thousand miles away. Everything paid out was eventually collected from Air India's insurers. Reardon Smith paid our out-of-pocket expenses; and we put away our files, by then over a foot thick.

Why do we do such things? It was nothing whatever to do with us. Partly it is on principle. The function of insurance is to help people. If an insurer has no legal liability to pay, he may still very often give advice and assistance. Partly, of course, it is good business. 'Cast thy bread upon the waters; for thou shalt find it after many days.' The next year, Reardon Smith insured three additional ships with us. I think, however, it is fair to say that when we took on that quite arduous task, such a consideration was not in our minds. We just did what we thought needed to be done.

4

Robbers and Pilferers

I have a friend who is by no means of the City of London bowler-hat type. Jack Carroll has been many years a docker in Bristol, like several generations of his family. Of Irish descent, he is as rugged as he looks. He is a natural leader of men. On the occasion when he took me round the Avonmouth docks, I was astonished how many men of all kinds hailed him by name. For years he was a bitter opponent of both management and the trade union officials. A friend and associate of the notorious Jack Dash, he was the leading spirit in the unofficial dockers' committee at Bristol, and some think he was intended to follow Dash as national leader of the unofficial shop stewards' movement. At the time of the big Bristol strike, he was called a 'wrecker' on television by the then Minister of Labour, Ray Gunter.

In fact, it is as well that Jack has had a basic change of heart, which began at a London meeting for men of industry sponsored by Moral Re-Armament—the first occasion when I grasped his horny hand. What gripped him there was not the presence of employers, but the words of militant trade unionists, some previously Communist Party members of long standing. They were still militants, but now for constructive ideas. Jack threw himself whole-heartedly into this new conception of revolution, that situations are changed by the change in people. And these new convictions have taken him to Australia, India, Brazil and other countries. Once, I travelled with him to France to speak together with him to port workers and management there.

Jack claims that change in people (including himself) has not merely affected labour relations, but many other issues. One of the problems he talks about is pilferage of cargo from the docks.

I will reproduce as far as I can remember his own picture of the problem.

'One of my mates on the docks was a great one for nipping stuff which came through our hands. All sorts of stuff. One day we were discharging frozen lambs from New Zealand. Lovely little chaps they were, and my mate said he'd made up his mind to nip one of them to take home.

'I told him not to be stupid. There was no chance of getting away with it, if he did; but he said he'd got it all figured out. He would bring his old car round and park it at the end of the shed near where we were working. Then, when we landed a sling-load of lamb carcasses, he could whip one out of the sling and into the boot of the car before anyone could wink. And so he did.

'But he'd missed one thing. The place he had put the car was overlooked by the management offices. I reckon someone looked out of the window at the wrong moment, and saw it all. He probably even noted the number of the car.

'When knocking-off time came, my mate drove off, but found extra police on the gate. He tried the side gate. Same there. A large copper put his hand up, and made him open up the boot of the car. "And what," he asked in a sarcastic way, "do you think you are doing with that lamb?" "Well, it's like this," says my mate, "I saw this little lamb, and I thought there must be something wrong with it. It's got no head or feet. So I'm taking it to the vet." ' The story had a sad ending in the magistrates' court.

A change in the attitudes of many dockers brought down pilferage at Bristol. It was needed, there as in other ports.

At one time, there passed across my desk many of the outturn figures for meat cargoes discharged in London and other British ports. The short deliveries were then running at from £1,800 to £4,000 or more a ship. And hundreds of cargoes came in each year. Much of the missing meat went out as joints under the coats of the dockers.

Some people, however, had more ambitious plans. A handful of notes were slipped to a tallyman by the driver of a meat delivery van, and the load was recorded as 80 sides of beef, instead of 90. At an unscheduled stop on the way to the depot, ten were delivered to the shop of an unscrupulous butcher. Many transactions of this

D

kind were eventually proved in the criminal courts. One butcher, caught in the act of receiving stolen meat, had in his possession a notebook recording many such deals, and the 'expenses' paid. Another time, as a delivery was being made to a shop in Portsmouth, a car pulled up. Out jumped detectives who had followed it 80 miles from the London docks. 'Where did you spring from?' asked an astonished thief.

All kinds of commodities are affected. At one time, three successive ships in a transatlantic service arrived in Britain with general cargo—thousands of packages in each. Each carried one small case of the synthetic 'flints' for cigarette lighters, worth thousands of pounds. All three disappeared without trace.

For years there were mysterious shortages of raw cotton in bales at Liverpool docks. Investigations produced nothing. Then it was found that loads were going out of the gates on cleverly forged passes. The police found that the marketing problem for this valuable stuff had been dealt with ingeniously but simply. A cotton broker, very advanced in years and no longer acute in mind, had been approached, allegedly by a cotton mill which (he was told) had more raw material at times than it could handle, and he had sold the stolen goods for the thieves on the Liverpool Cotton Exchange! A tightening of dock procedures put an end to that little game.

Another gang in Liverpool did very well until the discarded mistress of one thief took her resentment to the police and gave them names and addresses. At one house the garage was crammed with radios, perfumes, spirits and such.

In London, too, a gang operated a big scheme based on forged receipts for goods intended to be transhipped, and therefore shifted from one dock to another. Surprised by the police, they resisted violently, and one officer was badly injured. After a big manhunt, the leader was trapped in a telephone box in Epping Forest.

For every big thief, however, there are a thousand little ones. If these could be eliminated, the big criminals would find themselves more exposed and vulnerable. Perhaps the major problem is much more the men who stroll out of the dock gate with a length of silk wound round their bodies under their coats, or those who fit themselves out with new shoes from the cargo so that the ship arrives with the discarded old shoes littering the 'tween-deck, or the long-established custom in Glasgow of bumping down a case of whisky on its corner in a way which breaks the corner bottle, and holding a tin cup to catch what drains out.

The problem is, of course, not just a British problem. In Rio de Janeiro losses by pilferage in the nineteen fifties were on such a scale as to call for specially high insurance premiums on cargoes for Brazil. Losses and insurance premiums came down a great deal, following the same kind of change in men as affected Jack Carroll and his friends, and originating in the same way. I have met some of them, Nelson Marcellino do Carvalho, Damasio Cardoso, Othon Barbosa, and others. One of them, known as 'the king of thieves', estimated that he got away with an average of $400 U.S. worth of cargo every week. I told him my firm must have paid for some of the goods he stole. He roared with laughter and said (through an interpreter), 'Now I have changed, I am your greatest benefactor.'

The reduction in the pilferage level was only one of the changes in the port. The official trade union led by Nelson, and an unofficial and illegal one led by Damasio, had been fighting for control with pistols, knives and bottles. They merged into one, with officials publicly elected in a manner the Brazilian newspapers described as 'a model of democracy'. Political manipulation of the labour force and large scale corruption were neutralized. Strikes were greatly reduced. And the port began to show a regular profit.

I could tell many tales of cargo robberies elsewhere, in Montreal and New York, Adelaide and Genoa.

Just after the 1939-45 war the problem was so acute that the directors of our mutual insurance association decided something must be done about it, and told us (the managers) to prepare recommendations. Dawson Miller, our senior partner, threw the problem to me. I was, frankly, taken aback. Despite my constant endeavours to keep in touch with the ships, their owners, and their practical affairs, I was basically a desk man. How could I draft a programme for the men who ran the ships and their operations in many countries?

I gave the matter much thought, especially in those morning hours of listening for guidance from a source outside myself. There must be a plan against crime, and for order and the consideration of others. Eventually, I produced a draft of a single-page circular. It dealt with the matter entirely in terms of people—the choice of reliable supervisors, the encouragement of responsibility in everyone involved, the removal of temptation by making it difficult for the thieves. Dawson Miller's secretary typed out the draft for me, and I can remember her slapping it down on my desk and snorting, 'You might as well say straight out that the answer is Moral Re-Armament.' She surprised me. I had not seen it that way; but maybe she was more perspicacious than I, as well as blunt in her opinions.

Anyway, I put it forward to Dawson Miller. It was long after the days when my first attempts at business correspondence were scrawled over with alterations when I submitted them to him for approval; but I was agreeably surprised when he altered one word only, replacing a fanciful verb by a plain one. My draft was circulated at the next directors' meeting. They not only approved it unanimously, but asked all our competitors to join in issuing it as a joint circular to the shipowners from many countries whom we insured.

In the following months, pilferage went down and down. Whether 'my' circular had any connection with it, I cannot say; but I do know that some companies adopted practices recommended in the circular. One London liner firm instituted checking and security measures which cost them £70,000 a year, and found them to be a good investment.

Better tallying procedures were introduced. A director of a big stevedoring firm told me that if fuller details had to be recorded by the tally clerks (weights of items, for example), the results were always more accurate than with a simple running tally of the number of pieces or packages.

We began, too, certain security measures of our own, which obviously I cannot reveal. I can, however, say that they were carried out in close association with the police. A few years later, I heard that there was talk around the docks that 'the insurance companies are up to something, and we don't know what it is'. A very desirable reaction.

5

Some Cargo Disappears

Sometimes, of course, cargo just cannot be accounted for. Does it disappear? Or was it never shipped? Or was it delivered somewhere else?

The shipowner, through his crew or agents, acknowledges that he received it, but it is not there to be delivered. Failing some explanation, he has to pay and so therefore does his protecting and indemnity club. Many times I faced this kind of situation. Sometimes the mystery was solved. Sometimes (like the police in many kinds of crime) I was sure I knew, but could prove nothing. Sometimes I was completely baffled.

Consider the Scandinavian ship which brought a cargo of telephone poles from Finland to the London docks, and the consignees claimed 176 poles short. Why? It was hardly likely that a young seaman or stevedore would slip one under his coat as a present for his girl friend. And in this case, there was a complete discrepancy between the counts made by the timber merchants' tally-men on the quay, and a countercheck by members of the crew made as the poles were swayed up by the cranes over the ship's rail. The shore tally showed a shortage : the ship tally showed that all the cargo called for was delivered.

I had the ship's tally-books sent up to the office, and did a hurried check of them. They looked all right to me, small note books, with the tally made in the old well-known 'gate' system, of four vertical strokes with a fifth diagonally across them to indicate five units, totals at the end of each line, and a running total at the foot of each page. So we agreed to put the papers to an arbitrator to decide whether or not the claim for the missing poles should be paid.

He decided against us. Disappointing, indeed. A day or two

later, he called in to see me, and returned the papers. 'I thought,' he said, 'you would like to have another look at these tally books. First of all, on one of the later pages, the totals do not correspond with the number of gates. But there is something else. They are not suspiciously clean. In fact, they are as dirty as you would expect after hours of handling on the deck of a ship covered with dust and traces of oil and rust. But look at this.' He opened one of the books and put it face down on my desk. Spreading the fingers of one hand over the two covers, he twisted it back and around on the desk top. There were five round smudges on the cover, corresponding to the tips of his thumb and fingers. The book clearly had been artificially dirtied, rubbed in dirt, after it was written up.

The Scandinavians, reluctant to pay for cargo which doubtless had not been shipped (and carelessly counted at the loading port), had prepared books specially to show the wrong figures. All those 'gates' drawn for nothing.

It may seem hard that the shipowners (and thus we) paid for cargo which was never shipped, but they had given receipts for it, and the timber importers had paid on those receipts.

Another far larger discrepancy arose in a different way. After the Second World War, large quantities of army stores had to be brought back from Egypt to the United Kingdom. One ship arrived, to deliver a long list of all sorts of things, all except one item on the list—250 army trucks! But the explanation was simple. The Strick Line had an arrangement that their ships returning from the Persian Gulf should pick up anything they could find space for when they reached Port Said. The army people produced a bill of lading listing all they had ready for shipment. There was no room for the trucks, and someone just forgot to strike them off the list.

Then, a ship was chartered to carry a full cargo of guano (bird droppings) from the Seychelles to Durban for Fisons, the fertilizer people. The outturn showed a shortage of no less than 1,200 tons against the bill of lading figures. The usual enquiries turned up nothing at first. In the case of a cargo measured by weight, a fairly close check can be made by comparing the ship's draught before and after loading. Most people have seen the six-inch high figures, six inches apart, marking each foot of submersion, painted on both sides of the stem, and again on both sides of the ship aft. For a ship of this size, every fifty tons or so of cargo put her another inch deeper in the water. The captain, however, said that he had loaded off shore from barges, and the sea was too rough to measure the draught. He thought the bill of lading figure too high, but could only guess.

More detailed enquiries showed that the barges brought the cargo in bags, which shore labourers emptied into the holds. The first hundred or two were each weighed on deck, and the average weight had been multiplied by the thousands of bags emptied each day. It was fairly obvious that as the men got more tired (and perhaps more nauseated) they filled the bags less and less full. Certainly, the total in the bill of lading was a wholly unreliable figure; and this was one claim we did not pay.

For several generations a story has been told against the famous P. & O. Company. It could even be true. In the old days a stream of P. & O. ships carried general cargo of all kinds out to India and the East. On one of them a new chief officer was appointed, a conscientious man. One of his duties, of course, was (under the captain) the care of the cargo; and he took an early opportunity to inspect all the ship's holds, accompanied by the ship's boatswain and carpenter. If you have never been down the hold of a cargo ship, I can assure you that physically they had quite an arduous task. Access is by vertical steel-runged ladders, and even in a small cargo liner this means down and up thirty odd feet of ladder five or six times, and walking considerable distances in the holds and 'tween-decks. And every ship has a variety of equipment, pipes, drainage systems, and so on, everywhere.

In the corner of one hold there was a smallish wooden erection, painted grey like everything else, and the officer asked casually, 'What's that?' The carpenter replied, even more casually, 'Oh, just a casing to protect some valves on the pumping system.' They turned away, but the officer found himself thinking, 'Why there?' He turned back, and told the carpenter to prise off one of the planks, and check. With a shrug, he did so. Inside was a grand piano. It was much decayed. Years before, it had doubtless been overlooked in its distant corner, and recorded as short-delivered. There it had been ever since, and each time the hold had been painted, the packing case got painted as well.

Another story was told me by a P. & O. man. If there is a discrepancy in the loading tallies, as there was in the discharging tallies in the case of the telegraph poles discussed earlier, the usual practice is to issue a bill of lading for the smaller number, adding words such as '47 pieces more in dispute, if on board to be delivered'. My P. & O. friend told me with a straight face that they had in the office an old bill of lading acknowledging the loading of three live elephants, one more in dispute.

A Norwegian ship carried in wartime a cargo of miscellaneous stores for British troops in the Middle East, including canteen stores. The short deliveries, when she discharged at Basrah, included 577 cases of canned beer, each containing 48 cans. I felt this was rather beyond a joke, and insisted that the ship's managers obtained a special report from the captain. Eventually, there arrived from somewhere on the other side of the world a long report, which must have provided a pleasant occupation for a dull day at sea. It may be summarized as follows : 'I have made exhaustive enquiries as to the missing cases of beer. I find that, by a remarkable coincidence, all my officers on that voyage were total abstainers, so that there is no question of any of them being responsible. The lower-deck ratings were all Arabs, who are enjoined by their religion to abstain from alcohol. When the ship arrived at Basrah, the military authorities, on account of the nature of the cargo, put an armed guard on board to prevent pilferage by the local labour. These guards were assisted in their duties by volunteers from among their comrades. The climate in Iraq being so hot, it does occur to me that some of these guards may have had an occasional drink from the cargo, but I do not think this could have exceeded in all 100 cases, or 4,800 cans. As regards the balance, I cannot suggest any possible clue. It remains a mystery.'

Another interesting case also arose in that part of the world, at a port in Saudi Arabia. A ship arrived without a good deal of her deck cargo which the captain said had been washed overboard in a storm. The insurers of the cargo pointed out that meteorological reports (admittedly meagre) did not report any storm, and they were rude enough to suggest that the goods might have been sold off privately at a small port as the ship passed down the Red Sea. I may say that the ship was a small general trader, and the captain was part owner. The only way to avoid the shipowners paying £12,000 was to go to law at the remote port of destination. I made enquiries and found that the sole fount of justice in Saudi Arabia was the King, who delegated his powers to the local emirs. The emir would sit to hear cases at sunset, surrounded by his sheikhs. A complainant would state his case, and his adversary would reply. There would be a silence. Perhaps one of the sheikhs would quote from the Koran some passage that seemed to him relevant. There would be a further silence. When the emir felt this matter had been adequately considered, he would pronounce judgement.

It was permissible for a litigant who was foreign or who felt he needed help, to ask one of the sheikhs to present his case. We arranged for this to be done for the shipowner. The emir awarded the claimant £6,000, and a suitable fee was paid to the sheikh, perhaps £600—I do not remember. But I do remember reflecting that it could be considered a system at least as effective, just and civilized as our more complicated procedures in the West. It depends heavily on the integrity of the judge. So, of course, does our system.

There are many in shipowners' or marine insurers' offices who could talk for days of odd occurrences of this nature. But why do they arise? Human frailty, I suppose, is the answer. Wrongdoing sometimes, carelessness and stupidity at others. On one level, we as insurers did not object actively to the financial losses involved. There is an old saying in the insurance world, 'No claims mean no premiums', and we took a certain pride in paying for losses. On another level, the losses irk us continually; and insurers sporadically make drives to reduce losses. The cost of the losses, and of insurance against them, goes directly on to the cost of goods and services, and so on to the consumer. They represent waste of the world's resources.

It often seemed to me that one great defence would be a heightened sense of responsibility all round. I once attended a high-level conference on pilferage with shipowners, master stevedores, government officials, and representatives of the Port of London Authority. The P.L.A. men (not the present men, I feel sure) argued strongly that, whoever was to be held responsible for cargo losses, it was never, never, never the responsibility of the P.L.A. Their bye-laws, they said, made that clear. Yet they provided the premises and the police force for the docks, and employed directly some of the port labour. I was scandalized, and told them so.

In the early stages of the container traffic in Dublin three full containers disappeared entirely. My enquiries showed that there were no precautions of any kind, no fence, no watchmen, no records of receipts or deliveries. Changes were made, of course.

It would be better if the legal position was always such that people were accountable for their actions, or for improper inaction. In practice, contracts or statutes constantly interfere with this situation. Such and such a person, or body, is not responsible for this, that and the other. A lot of my business life consisted in sorting out such tangles. But it is not always essential that you or I stand strictly on our rights if it means evading a moral responsibility. This can apply even when we are acting on behalf of someone else, a trust, or shareholders.

Perhaps I should cull an example from my own experience, once again. The mutual insurance association my firm manages has in its conditions of insurance a clause which is, I believe, unique to this type of insurance, the shipowners' P. and I. 'clubs'. Beside all the risks set out in the cover, there is a clause (sometimes called the 'omnibus clause') whereby the directors may reimburse an insured shipowner for any loss or expense incident to shipowning which the directors in their sole discretion consider should be paid. As I have written elsewhere, an example was where a ship in an emergency had to carry a crowd of dockers off to another port. The directors agreed to pay for their food on board, and their fares back.

With us, the principle of going beyond the letter of the law is written down as a possibility; but in any business there is usually some basis on which it can be applied, if necessary. A Yorkshire friend of mine, Farrar Vickers, was for years chairman and managing director of a family oil business. The firm got into a dispute with another firm, and after a long fight won the battle. Yet Farrar had the clear conviction that he should yield the point, and pay up. He never regretted it, and has always regarded it as a good business decision.

If there were a greater readiness in us all to say 'this is my responsibility', a vast range of things which now go wrong might well not do so.

6

Dockers, Ports and Containers

My job sometimes spotlighted the sins of dockers, but I have been lucky enough to meet some of them, and at least begin to understand their sterling qualities, too.

In England they may be dockers or stevedores, and there are several views as to the difference between the two. One (and I hasten to say that I do not know if it is the correct one) is that stevedores work on the ships, and dockers on the quay. In the United States they are 'longshoremen', in Australia 'wharfies', although the Union's title refers to Waterside Workers. In Rio de Janeiro and in Brooklyn black and white dockers work amicably together. In Famagusta, Cyprus, they had Greek and Turkish dockers in the same gang, until the whole Greek population fled from the city.

Dockers have much in common the world over. They tell you that one of them in London, loading cased cargo, dropped his wallet down the narrow space between the cargo and the ship's side. He drew an arrow on the plating, and wrote 'Wallet dropped here', signing it 'TGWU' and his union membership number. It came back from the Australian union with its contents untouched.

The other London union, the Amalgamated Stevedores and Dockers, called the 'blue' union from the colour of its membership cards, finds that its men are treated as honorary members of the Australian union. The reason is that long, long ago, when the Australians were in a drawn-out strike, the London union sent encouragement and funds.

There is something different, something special about the men of the docks. Partly it is a heritage of the suffering of the distant past. Twenty or thirty years ago I met an old chap of 70 or so, still working as a lighterman. In those days, the lighters were a far more important factor in moving cargo about London's docks and river than they are today; but those 'swim' barges, with their unique design, are still familiar to us. There had been labour trouble, and the lightermen's union was operating a 'go slow' in support of a wage claim. The port was choked with ships.

We met at a hall in dockland after a showing of a play called *The Forgotten Factor*, sponsored by Moral Re-Armament, a play based on actual incidents of change in men in industry, both employers and workers. I said to him : 'Could you explain to me what is really behind this trouble on the river?' He looked me in the eye for a moment, then down at his big hands gripping his knees as he sat, silent for a bit, and then began : 'Well, mister, it's like this. A long time ago, when I was a little nipper, the port was out on strike. My dad was out. There was no money in the house. There was no dole in those days, no public assistance. You might get something from the parish, if you was lucky, and my dad went off to see. All he could get was one loaf of bread. There was ten of us at home. He put it on the kitchen table, and we all gathered round. He got the bread knife and cut it in half, and it was green mould all through.' That was all he would say.

On the basis of cold reason, that sixty-year-old memory was utterly irrelevant to the conditions of today, to powerful trade unions, full employment (as we had at that time), and welfare payments for all in need. But you could almost smell that loaf in the air, and the fear that such times might come again one day. I could understand it a little. My mother's grandfather was a baker in Stepney, near the docks. She had known real poverty in childhood, in Southwark and the New Kent Road. I had to live, with my wife, penny by penny when we were first married, in three rooms at the top of a house off Brixton Hill.

In many countries across the world, you will find the worst slums near the docks, because in that area there was work when a ship was in, and none when there was no ship to be worked.

Once too, in 1945, when he was eighty-five years old, I had tea with the legendary Ben Tillett, who led the famous battle for the 'Dockers' Tanner' in (I think) 1889, the strike which lifted dockers' pay to no less than sixpence an hour—forty hours of work for a single pound. He told me how, as a lad, he once walked twelve miles to Tilbury, got four hours' work at threepence an hour, and walked twelve miles home. Most of the shilling must have been used up in boot leather.

For so many years, too, all the dockers had to arrive in the early morning, 'on the stones', to see if the foremen would pick them for that day's work. If not, there was nothing. It was a degrading business.

It is all very different from today's docker, who is quite likely to drive himself to work from an outer suburb. Yet many remember low wages, and old stories are still re-told. These things colour feelings; and the threat of losing what is nowadays a good job may provoke resistance which has a trace of desperation with its emotional origin generations back.

Another characteristic of port workers is their intense loyalty to each other. It transcends reason. On one occasion, there was a strike of stevedores and dockers in London; and there had been speculation whether other workers, such as lightermen and employees of ship-repairers, would come out in sympathy. A ship-owner told me that he had a ship repairing at the London Graving Dock at the time. A gang was at work in the engine room, and the owner's engineer superintendent had looked in to see how they were progressing. While he was there, a young lad clattered down the iron ladder and gave a piece of paper to the charge-hand, who looked at it and called out to the gang: 'Pack up. We're going ashore.' As they were gathering up their tools, the superintendent asked: 'What's all this about?' The charge-hand replied: 'No idea, mister. This is all I know,' and showed him the piece of paper. It was just a blank piece of grubby paper bearing only the scribbled words, 'All out.' Looked at from one angle, the attitude of the men was half-witted. Looked at from another, as loyalty, or working-class solidarity, it was sublime.

It is no wonder that dockers have a long history of totally following the leaders thrown up by themselves. Thus in many cases unofficial leaders have brought the majority of dockers into conflict with authority, including their own union officials. In Britain there has been for decades an unofficial movement of locally elected shop stewards (and others), which acts more or less independently of the national union officials. Their influence

fluctuates. Sometimes they seem to control the major ports; sometimes they are not heard of for a period. Some but not all are
from the extreme left in politics, Communist, Trotskyite, and
so on.

The peak of their influence was probably in 1951, when London
and other ports were totally paralysed for many weeks in a strike
which began as action in sympathy with a strike by Canadian
merchant seamen. The London unofficial committee even published its own news-sheet at that time. I have known for years the
'business manager' of that news-sheet, Jack Manning; and, long
after he decided that to support constructive ideas was more
exciting and satisfying than wrecking tactics, he would still recall
with relish, 'Our paper made the Communist *Daily Worker* read
like the London *Times*.'

Fortunately, loyalty can equally produce support for reasonable
men and sensible policies, especially if they are put forward boldly
by one of themselves. A man I know was a spectator at a mass
meeting of dockers on Tower Hill in London. Its aim was to
extend for a further period a strike which was really only serving
the political ends of a few extremists. The leaders, extremists to
a man, were on the back of an open lorry with a microphone, and
their fiery speeches were raising the temperature in (to them) a
very satisfactory manner. A docker in the crowd, at the end of
one speech, called out: 'Is this a democratic meeting?' There
could be only one answer from the platform, 'Yes'. He then
shouted: 'Can I come up on the platform and speak?' Again
there was only one possible answer. He took over the microphone
and said: 'I don't agree with what our brothers here have been
saying,' and went on to explain why he felt the strike was not in
the workers' interests. At the end of his speech, most of the crowd
drifted off to work, and the meeting was abandoned.

In some countries, leadership of the port unions has been a
key to power for various types of men. It may be political or
revolutionary power, or the power from corruption and crime,
or both types together, as has been known in some South American
ports. It is widely said that the Mafia controls or controlled the
unions in some U.S. ports; and on the west coast of North
America, power has long been in the hands of the Australian-
born Harry Bridges and his Communist colleagues.

There is, however, no reason why dockers should be led by those with ulterior motives, whether corrupt or revolutionary, and there are many sound leaders across the world. One such is Jim Beggs, president of the dockers' union in Melbourne, and known for his positive ideas and active association with Moral Re-Armament. A few years back, he visited the principal British ports, and was interviewed by *Lloyd's List*, the oldest daily newspaper in the world, owned and published by the Committee of Lloyd's. One story he told in that front-page article was of meeting the chairman of the port employers at a certain port. Beggs asked him what the ordinary dockers felt about conditions in the port. 'I've never met an ordinary docker,' replied the employer, 'I only deal with their full-time union officials.' Jim thought this was crazy, and said so; and I heard later that the employer had started going down on the quayside so as to meet individual workers.

The Australian ports used to be completely communist-controlled, with constant labour disputes. Some of us can remember how one group, discharging sanitary toilet fixtures, demanded extra pay as 'embarrassment money'. A shipowner told me once he had just had a ship take 118 days to discharge a cargo in Australia and load another. And to add to industrial occasions for strikes, it has been common to call strikes against ships trading with or carrying the flags of countries politically unpopular with the extreme left. Now things are far more rational on the Australian coast, and this is largely due to men like Beggs.

Beggs was in England again in 1975, and told me that when he was first elected it was union policy never to meet employers except across a conference table during a dispute. The union leaders were invited to an official function. Jim said he was going, and there was quite a row because 'the bosses' had also been asked. Jim said the union men had as much right to be there as the bosses, and went. The general secretary (a communist) and some others still follow their old rule, but most of the officials are now quite prepared to rub shoulders with employers off duty. And that general secretary supported Beggs for re-election as president.

It was during the Second World War, when Ernest Bevin was

Minister of Labour and National Service, and when the British dockers performed tremendous tasks often in dangerous conditions, that the first plans were made for guaranteed employment for them, or rather for a guaranteed minimum wage, whether there was work or not. There was much to be said for the principle. The National Dock Labour Scheme has, however, been clumsy, cumbersome and costly. The proof of this has been the rapid transfer of trade to ports where the Scheme does not apply, and even to ports in other countries. During the great European coal shortage some twenty-five years ago, coal imports from the U.S.A. to Britain were to a large extent carried first to Rotterdam, and then in smaller ships to a wide range of U.K. ports where they would be discharged cheaper and quicker than in the ports covered by the Dock Labour Scheme.

As I write, it is proposed to apply the National Dock Labour Scheme to all ports and all cargo handling within some miles of the ports. Technically, it seems a disaster to me. The chairman of commissioners of a small, ancient and efficient port told me they had only thirty regular port workers. There was work for them most days, and overtime sometimes. They liked it that way, he said. He knew most of them by name himself. To bring places like that into a huge and complex national system seems incomprehensible. The same applies to handling of cargo in warehouses, cold stores, and so on, in the areas round ports. That is all intended to be 'dock work'.

The only people who really win with great centrally controlled systems are those who are working for a totalitarian society. I say this although I am sure that some who support the Labour Government's port scheme do so for another reason, though perhaps with some of them it is more a pretext.

The introduction of containers for the carriage of much cargo has produced a series of violent disputes between dockers and employers, and even between rival unions or sections of the same union. There have been strikes, walk-outs, boycotts, dockers refusing to handle containers 'stuffed' inland, lorry-drivers who carry the containers picketing against dockers, and enough violence to produce criminal convictions. All these were spectacularly reported by the press, and exploited for political purposes.

Clearly, years of industrial guerrilla warfare in a sensitive area

E

such as the ports cannot be tolerated. Dockers have argued (both in Britain and the United States) that the stuffing and stripping of containers should be treated as dock work, even if it is done hundreds of miles from the sea, since only dockers, they say, can pack goods securely for the strains of sea passage. At one time, at certain ports, containers packed inland were solemnly unpacked and re-packed on the quayside before despatch. Yet the whole basis of the container concept is to reduce the number of times goods are handled and to speed up transport.

More recently, dockers in Hull succeeded in delaying for a long time an experiment called BACAT, involving barges full of cargo carried in a specially constructed ship to and from which they were floated on inland waterways, because 'it took work away from the dockers'. There have been protests, too, about containers going by the Trans-Siberian Railway from Japan to Europe as being a threat to the conventional pattern of trade.

However sympathetic one feels towards people who lose their jobs, I see no reason why any person should have an absolute right to do the same job for the whole of his life. It is a reversion to the thinking behind the Luddite riots, the machine-smashing at the beginning of the Industrial Revolution. And in this century changes come so quickly in all fields that clinging to old ways is even more obviously wrong than two hundred years ago.

If management and workers do not change with the times, progress will pass them by. Other countries will sprint ahead of ours. We need maximum flexibility and experiment in port and transport methods; and for this we need a minimum of centralization.

If things are not going well in some field or other, there are many today whose reaction is, 'The government must do something. Bring in a law. Stop this. Subsidize that. Appoint a commission of enquiry. Regulate. Control. Forbid.' I do not believe this is the British way. It is not the human way either. We are supposed to be able to choose between right and wrong, all of us.

I have a strong faith in the infinite capacity of the human brain and spirit, if given a chance. It may be bathos, it may be trivial, but I would like to tell one other story about the British dockers. Just after the Second World War the MacAndrews Line bought the ex-German motorship *Empire Dove* to supplement their fleet carrying general cargo between the U.K., Spain and the Mediterranean. I was invited to lunch on board, and I asked the captain how they got on loading in the London docks. 'The men at our berth are marvellous,' he said; and went on to describe an incident when he was discharging at Barcelona on the previous voyage. The foreman of the stevedores came up on to the bridge to see the captain and chief officer, and complained that they were unable to get certain vehicles out of the 'tween-decks. These spaces were only about eight feet high, and the strengthening girders round the hatches took up further space. There were several trucks stowed in one 'tween-deck, and the Spaniards could not get them under the overhead beams. 'Have you tried letting the tyres down a bit?' asked the captain. 'Yes, we've done that, and it's not enough.' The chief officer looked at the captain and said: 'I think I know the ones they mean, sir. Would you like to come below and see?' They followed each other down the ladders to where the Spanish stevedores were standing and sitting around. 'Yes, I saw them loaded in London,' said the chief officer. 'It's quite simple really. Get thirty or forty men to hang on to each truck. Their weight will flatten out the springs, and they'll just go under.'

This sort of skill is dying out as new methods are introduced. Cargo is loaded and discharged by grabs, suction tubes, conveyors, or in giant containers, so that machines do almost all the work. The old methods are going, and the number of men required diminishing. But the new skills are equally fascinating.

A strong rearguard action has been fought against changes, and the details of this make it plain how stupid it has been. For example, not so many years ago a certain British shipowner told a group of us of visits to two British ports, one in England, one in Wales, as a result of dissatisfaction he felt over the discharge of iron ore. At the English port, large grabs were used, and the shipowner climbed to the cab of the crane to watch. 'What are all those stevedores doing on the deck?' he asked the crane-driver. 'It looks dangerous to me. They might be hit by the grab.'

The driver replied: 'We have to keep the same number of men on board as we used to when we used buckets. Then they were in the hold, filling the buckets. Now, all they have to do is to go down and shovel the last few tons to where my grab can reach it.' He added, with some feeling : 'They get paid a piece-work rate according to how fast I get the cargo out with my grab. And at a higher rate than I get.'

The shipowner went on to the Welsh port. After watching their methods he said to the port manager : 'This is better than what I saw yesterday. You don't have all those men on deck hanging round doing nothing.'

'No,' said the port manager, 'we stopped that. It was dangerous. But the union still insists on full gangs, and I can't start working a ship until the right number of men have been counted into the rest room we built to keep them out of the way and out of the rain.'

These absurd abuses have, I believe, been corrected now; but there are others still about.

Resistance to change may come from real or imaginary fears of being without a job. It may come from a trade union's desire not to lose membership and authority. An official of the International Longshoremen's Association in the U.S.A. told me that containerization was a desperate issue for them. The union had guaranteed pensions and medical care to a lot of retired workers, and were having to put the financing of it on to a membership which had already declined by nearly half.

Another factor must in some cases be management men who do not look ahead. If new methods are coming, it is essential to foresee their consequence in human terms. How will they affect the people now working? One company introduced a container service between Melbourne and Hobart. They knew that with the quick loading and discharge there would only be stevedoring work at Hobart on perhaps two days a week. They made a special agreement with the trade union whereby a certain number of men would be permanently employed. If not required for loading and discharging, they would do maintenance and other work, including repairing and painting containers.

This was a small-scale affair; but equally good arrangements have been made elsewhere for bigger operations. In Bristol, for example, Jack Carroll (whom I mentioned earlier) took part in negotiations which settled manning and pay for discharging packaged (as opposed to loose) timber before the first cargo left Canada. And the dockers discharged it in record time.

I hope reason will prevail, and that throughout our ports, large and small, we can preserve maximum scope for human ingenuity and for consideration of the individual.

7

Education

I did not suddenly materialize in St Mary Axe, the street which is the centre of the world of ships; nor was I born, full grown, in a grey suit and a stiff white collar, from the wake of a steamer in the Pool of London, or the muddy tracks of a London bus, in the same general way as (but rather unlike) Botticelli's Venus. I had, of course, the usual background of birth and growth, family and school. And some aspects of these must have deeply affected my business life. It may be interesting to guess at some of them.

The background itself was not materially different from that of millions of others—the South London suburbs, and a life above the poverty line, but not much above it. A father, a mother, two brothers, a sister. Elementary schooling from the age of five at the standard type of state school.

Some things about my family may be noted, as definitely likely to influence my character, whether heredity or environment is the force we are looking at.

My father claimed to have one hundred per cent Irish blood, on the ground that his grandfather, who came to England about 1825, and his father both went back to Ireland long enough to find good Irish girls to marry. We used to think his Irish claims, including the estate and the old family, were just yarns spun to amuse us, until first my elder brother and then others of us went across, years later, saw Ledwithstown House in County Longford, and met genuine Irish Ledwiths. The estate, alas, was sold out of the family in 1904, and the house is slowly falling into ruin. Someone from the Georgian Society of Ireland once telephoned to me to ask if there were any chance of the Ledwiths returning to restore the house, but I had to say 'No'. However, it does seem, according to all the authorities I have seen, that Ledwiths have been around in West Meath and County Longford since about A.D. 1200. It may even be that the earliest arrived with the Geraldines in the first big invasion from Norman England in 1179. There has been trouble in Ireland ever since.

Suffice it that my father, though he never set foot in Ireland, had some of the qualities we associate with the Irish, the humour, the quick temper quickly over, the unpredictable response to circumstances, the mixture of irresponsibility with shrewdness. I have known him spring at me across a room with a carving knife in his fist. I was terrified; but I am sure he would never have used it. He worked for many years for a small printing and stationery business in Holborn. He described himself as a commercial traveller, but he seemed to dabble in all aspects of the business. When he was fifty it was bought up by a larger firm, which applied more rigid and doubtless effective procedures. I think he made little attempt to adapt himself to this, and soon he was discharged at a month's notice. At a time when trade was very bad, his reaction was to start on his own, with a tiny office in London, in association with a jobbing printer in the suburbs. For four years he nearly starved, I think, but eventually he built up a valuable little business, mainly by doing things a little better than other people. During the war, when labour, paper and everything was in very short supply, he used as an advertising slogan, 'We refuse to join the cult of cant'.

Before this, when he was still at the old firm, he was always questing for ways to add to his very modest salary and commission, by this private deal and that. The best deal he ever did, he would chucklingly tell his friends, was with a big job lot of carbon paper for typing; and he bought it from a Jew and sold it to a Scotsman! A more ambitious project was to rent two shops in the Walworth Road and put his brother in as manager. Father worked on the accounts himself in the evenings. The shops never paid their way in those lean years between the two world wars. Then the lease expired, and the landlord wanted to triple the rent. Dad could not possibly afford it. His response to the problem was to scrape together his last fifty pounds to pay for an option to buy the shops outright at a certain figure, any time in the next six months. Then he sought around; and just before the time expired he found a buyer at a higher figure. The difference paid off all his creditors, with a balance over.

He was consistently Conservative in politics, and served as a councillor in the great borough of Lambeth; but as chairman of the housing committee he pioneered in providing subsidized homes for the elderly poor, a project some would call socialistic.

As in many families, Mother probably had a greater effect on us children, if only through spending more time with us. But she was also a considerable personality. She was brought up in 'the Borough', which means Southwark. Her father had a shop near the spot from which Dan Chaucer's pilgrims in the Tales set off for Canterbury. If she liked, she could talk as Cockney as the best of them, but she would remind us to pronounce our intial *h*'s by a jingle :

> ''Ide me, 'ide me,' said the 'are, with all the 'ounds and 'arriers a-'urrying up be'ind 'im.
> ''Umbug,' says the 'edge-'og, and aimed 'alf an 'obnail at 'is 'ead, which made 'im 'op 'orrible.

Normally, however, she spoke beautifully, wrote a clear and elegant hand, and none of us can remember her making an error in spelling or arithmetic. Yet she left school at twelve years old, when her mother's illness and death made it needful for her to take on responsibility for the home and a baby sister.

Perhaps this was what made her feel passionately about education. She persistently kept all four of us at our studies in every way she could. In those days primary education was free to all up to the age of about fourteen, but secondary education was only available if you could pay (as we could not), or if the child could win a competitive scholarship to a secondary school. In the result, we all achieved something, one brother to a secondary school and thence by scholarship to university, my sister to secondary school and then to a teachers' training college, and my young brother and I to Christ's Hospital—of which more later.

Besides this, she unceasingly toiled to cook for us, feed us, keep us tidy, teach us manners and drag us to church, despite the fact that Dad never went there except on ceremonial occasions. I think she loved the services, and singing, and the social aspects, too. She was no saint, but she had a real faith. After she died (at ninety-one) someone said of her that she had the greatest of Christian virtues, in that, however bad her mood or circumstances might be, she could go quietly away, spend some minutes on her knees, and get up a different person.

I remember little significant from my years at Infants and Elementary schools, except perhaps that long snowfight one winter afternoon with the boys from a nearby school, when after two hours or more of snowballing we drove them right back to their home territory. And of course Mother's interview with the formidable headmistress, Miss Smith, about the examinations for secondary education. Parents had been asked to fill in a card saying, 'In the event of your child being successful, would you agree to his/her being considered for a scholarship to Christ's Hospital, or to Bancroft School? Answer Yes or No.' Mother went to the school to ask what it meant. Both were boarding schools, of charitable foundation, but Miss Smith added with freezing scorn, 'It doesn't matter what you say. This year there isn't a child in the school capable of a secondary school scholarship, let alone Christ's Hospital or Bancroft.'

Since my elder brother had won a scholarship a year or so before, Mother was most incensed at the slur on her second son. Her pressure on me to prepare adequately for the examination became intense, and she was delighted when many children proved the Head wrong by winning scholarships, including two of the twelve places to Christ's Hospital financed by London County for the whole of London's millions.

In due course, I arrived at the spreading grounds and huge brick buildings in Sussex, where Christ's Hospital gives 800 boys the same sort of education as is given at what the British, in their odd way, call public schools, Eton, Harrow, Winchester and the rest. The one great characteristic of this 400-year-old school is that it is still completely true to its charitable foundation. No boy can get in (or girl into the companion girls' school) unless his parents have a very modest income, and are thus deemed in need of help.

In those days, sport played a dominating part in deciding a boy's standing with other boys. My bad eyesight was a handicap in this. Even in Rugby football I could not see the ball at any distance. I just followed the crowd. At cricket I was hopeless, but enjoyed it.

The school was organized by houses: there were two big boarding-houses for the 120 boys from 9 to 11, and fourteen others which each housed 50 boys from 11 years upwards. The fourteen houses each played cricket and Rugby against all the others, at various levels of age and skill. In the last of my six years, I achieved the house first fifteen for Rugby. In cricket, I never got beyond the house third eleven.

Perseverance in difficulty was about the only thing I learnt from school sports. In fact, at Rugby football the one notable thing I ever did was in my very first game, in circumstances which made the event totally unmemorable for any one else but me. It was a friendly game against another house, for beginners, the very smallest boys. They were far better than us, and beat us by a large score. In fact, we only once got in a real attack, and in that the ball went loose over their line. Their full back, disdaining the safe play of touching the ball down, gathered it, and proceeded to clear it with a prodigious kick. Virtually the whole of our team was enthusiastically following up the ball, with me, breathless and short-sighted, in the middle somewhere. The kick was too low, the ball hit me in the pit of the stomach, I clutched it, and fell over the line, completely winded. It took minutes to revive me, but that try was our only score in the game.

The full back, T. N. Pearce, grew up to be an England international at Rugby, and later an international referee, and also captained Essex in the county cricket championship for a number of years.

Bullying was said to be dying out at Christ's Hospital then, but in my early years I seemed to attract a lot of it. Most of it was at the level of annoyance, but it sometimes went beyond. One bigger boy kicked me one morning to the extent that a master found me on the stairs, unable even to crawl to the top to get to the classroom. I found that the best defence was usually to show a completely impassive face, to be silent and unresisting. Then the bullies lost interest. But perhaps a more valuable lesson was to find a feeling of horror at myself rising in me when the bullying urge rose in me. It has not, I fear, always stopped me, but it does make me hate it in myself.

The monastic quality of boarding-school life in those days (it was 1918 to 1924) with practically no contact with girls in any way was with me an advantage rather than otherwise in dealing with the inevitable challenge of sex. It may have made me awkward when I came to mix with girls later, but it was an awkwardness which often held me back from acts I would have regretted afterwards.

The arguments in favour of sexual permissiveness leave me totally unconvinced. Some would say I am full of repressions and conflicts, and they might be right. But what are *they* repressing, and what conflicts do they have? Nothing has shaken in me the conviction, at first instinctive, that some things in this field are right and natural, and some are wrong and unnatural. The latter particulars include anything in which a person is self-centred, or in which one person exploits another for selfish reasons. When I have done wrong, or thought of doing so, I have mostly known it was wrong. When I left school at seventeen, I was only partly informed about sex, and rather scared of the whole business. However, I would think such a condition better than that of a seventeen-year-old I met later on who said that he had slept with thirty-one women of all sorts, and was fed up with the whole business.

It is true that I had no satisfying answer to problems or urgent feelings; and it was only later that I learnt of a power which by its nature was stronger than animal desire. One way I heard it put was, 'Sex is the second most powerful force in the world. The most powerful is the Spirit of God.' At seventeen this would have had no meaning for me; so I had to make do with what I had.

A thing which was sheer gain at school was to discover the joy of reading and to some extent the joy of learning. The academic level was good. Admittedly, the only important examination I ever passed at C.H. was the old 'London Matriculation', long since superseded, but I passed this with ease. At many schools it was a barrier to be braved, but with us the curriculum and teaching level were such that it was thought a disgrace to fail.

Reading for pleasure was far more important to me. The thrill is still vivid to me of my first encounters with H. G. Wells, Conrad, and Kipling. When we were studying Alaska and the Yukon, the head geography master, T. K. Mortimer-Booth, recommended us to read as background Jack London's *Smoke Bellew* and *White Fang*. There was John Buchan, too. Surely *The Three Hostages* came out first as a daily serial story in some paper. Was it the *Daily Mail*? They called that sort of serial a 'feuilleton', and it was printed in small type across the foot of one page introduced by a short summary of previous instalments. I seem to remember searching eagerly for it in our day-room newspapers.

The house library was mostly fiction, but in the school library I began to explore also history, biography, the *Mabinogion* and books on myths and legends.

The unspoilt Sussex countryside was another attraction on Sunday afternoons and on rare holidays. This led to an odd privilege. Three of us ventured into the grounds of Knepp Castle, a great country-house, chanced on the baronet and his wife and daughter, and were invited to tea several times as a result. Tennis, boats on the lake, and other pleasures were thrown in, totally undeserved. Why us three, out of 800 boys?

On the other hand, what I thought equally undeserved punishment visited me. Each year a large part of the school were entertained to tea by the Lord Mayor of London, that City where the school had been for 350 years. It was a stimulating excursion, with special trains each way. When we left the Mansion House, the Lord Mayor gave each boy a shilling, and the Lady Mayoress added a bag of buns. One year, on the train to London, the boys in our compartment decided that each should be tossed on to the luggage rack in turn. In the ensuing struggle, as I was in mid-air, I inadvertently grabbed the chain of the emergency alarm. The train stopped, a little disappointingly, in a station. The cause was traced, and in due course I suffered six cuts of the cane on my behind from my housemaster. It was light punishment compared with the paralysing possibility of the railway company's fining me. It might have been £5, an astronomical sum; but the company accepted my housemaster's report of his action in full satisfaction.

The grab at the communication cord was a pure accident. I felt aggrieved at the punishment, but this quickly passed, because for the first time I became reasonably popular at school. Looking back on my six years there, it sometimes seems that this exploit was my only achievement in the eyes of my contemporaries, my only claim to distinction. Truly, 'there ain't no justice'.

It reminds me of a talk with a young naval officer many years later. He told me of a colleague of his who had been court-martialled and reprimanded for an indiscretion ashore which had landed him in a Spanish jail for a night. A minor court-martial, they considered, was actually the best road to promotion. The admirals and other powers-that-be would say to each other: 'What about this candidate here? Brown—the name seems familiar. He must be a good man, or else I wouldn't remember his name.'

Of what I learnt in the class-room, very little seemed to be of direct use when I emerged into that other world where one had to earn a living. At one time I thought that geography was the one subject which was of some value in a business like ours. At the end of my school career, I specialized in mathematics, with a view to a future as an actuary in life insurance. (This plan failed when I landed in quite a different type of insurance.) During my last year I was doing 20 out of 32 'periods' each week (a period being 40 or 45 minutes) on mathematics, plus a similar proportion of evening work. Most of this I have never used and long since forgotten. I tried to introduce logarithms into the office, but it was quite pointless. In the office of today, with computers and calculators everywhere, it hardly seems necessary to be able to count on one's fingers—but of course it is.

In actual fact, there have been situations throughout my life when I wished I remembered more, and knew more, of most of the things we studied. A knowledge of history helps one to understand today's situation in many countries. An insurance man, like many other people, often needs the basics of chemistry and physics. And so it goes on.

But the greatest treasures which I found in the class-room I probably least regarded—speech and writing. French and German were not, I think, well taught. I did get a French prize, but it was by the simple method of being the only boy not promoted at the end of the term before. I did the whole term's work a second time, and rather naturally knew it better than the newcomers. In the 1920s, it is true that we used foreign languages little in our business, but the world is smaller now, and any grade of speaking or

writing the more common languages is a distinct asset. Not long
before I retired, I did a survey of the languages spoken reasonably
fluently by one or more people in the office. The list began with
French and German, of course, and ended (in order of numbers
who could speak them) with Swahili, Hindi, Estonian and Welsh.
I asked one young executive whether he or a colleague spoke
better Swahili. He considered, and said : 'I think mine is purer
in accent, but he knows more rude words.'

The poor French and worse German I learnt at school have
been used to the uttermost *circonflexe* and *Umlaut*. I have often
surprised myself with what came up from my sub-conscious mind,
as when I faced at Orly airport an enquiries girl who (believe it
or not) spoke no word of anything but French. I cannot sustain
a conversation in either language. My daughter says, more in pity
than in criticism, that I cannot complete a sentence in French
without at least two mistakes; but I can often understand a
Swede's carefully chosen German, or a Dutchman's carefully
chosen French. I have conversed with Jugoslavs, for example, in a
mixture of French and German fragments, plus a great deal of
hand signals. And people like it if you make an effort in their
language, even if it's only *Dobra dan* or *Arigato*.

The even greater asset was to have learnt to speak and write
English, not very well, I admit, but enough to be understood, and
with a sound enough foundation to be built on, brick by brick,
ever since. I was interviewed about my first book *Ships That Go
Bump in the Night* on BBC Radio 4, and one question was,
'What have you written before this?' I answered : 'Two insurance
policies and a bill of lading.' That question and answer were
edited out of the broadcast, but, if I had considered for a bit,
I might have added, 'A few newspaper articles, a score of technical pamphlets and a management training handbook, plus over
200,000 business letters.'

It is a sad thing that a good number of today's young people,
after what is supposed to be their education, cannot express themselves clearly in speech or writing. It is a factor which must mesh
in some way with that problem in industrial relations we constantly hear about—the failure in communication. And if anyone doubts that there is widespread failure in this field, he should
listen thoughtfully to a 'phone-in' radio programme or to one of

those television exercises where they stop people in the street and ask them questions. The proportion who cannot form a sentence is quite large; and I imagine that in both media those less eloquent still are quietly erased from the programme before it is broadcast.

I am therefore grateful that at Christ's Hospital I was made to read good English prose and verse out loud, and to write essays and other exercises. The school has a long literary tradition. Several of the boys' boarding-houses are named after 'old-boy' writers of the past, of whom Coleridge, Lamb, and Leigh Hunt are the best-known. And recent generations of boys have not been exactly barren of talent. Not everyone likes Bernard Levin. I suspect it is part of his policy to be so controversial as to provoke dislike in many. But there is no doubt as to his ability to form opinions and communicate them, in the press or on television.

However, the final test of education, so I am told, is whether it teaches you to learn. As to this, one cannot tell if oneself has the quality or not, but I am still very deeply conscious of the need to learn. I love to hear people (almost anyone) speaking of subjects they really know, and I sometimes retain at least a crumb or two of their knowledge. I like to try to understand people. Much of my reading is, I fear, of a rather trifling kind, but I like to mix in more serious books. Perhaps, too, this is one reason which, day by day, draws me so strongly to make attempts to find the leading of that 'inner voice' which all of us have.

I am grateful to Christ's Hospital, even though retrospection includes lonely and unhappy hours. It was a school with standards, and if you did not measure up to them, you knew it, whether or not active steps were taken to impress it on you.

Loyalty was taken for granted. In the one year in which I reached the house Rugby team, we won the League Cup, beating more of the other houses than any other. We were a light team in experience and ability, but our captain bought enough rope for each of us to skip two hundred times every night, and had us out to run a mile before breakfast every morning. We won most of our matches in the last ten minutes.

I learnt something about getting on with people from many different backgrounds, and something about how to deal with adversity and unpleasant situations. (The more difficult problem of how to deal with success was reserved for later.)

When I arrived in the City my brother, eighteen months older, was already at University College, London. For a time I was very jealous of him, especially as I knew he had many talents I could not match. Then I started telling myself that I was learning as much as he, anyway. I hope I was right. He went on to become an international figure in his field of industrial chemistry, but I suppose I did also, to some extent, in my field.

I have written elsewhere of Dawson Miller, the inspired chief who pulled my firm out of the ruck into an unmatched position in its particular sphere. I still wonder how he saw in me, a somewhat loutish youth of seventeen, a useful lieutenant for the future.

Outside the office, my sport and passion was cycle-touring. On Saturdays, when things were a little quieter and some of the seniors were not there, I would cycle up to the office. It saved me a tenpenny return bus fare, as well as being more enjoyable. If I was lucky when the lift came down, I would swing my bicycle in between the rattling gates before Jim Prince, the testy hunchbacked liftman, could stop me. If he was too quick, I carried it up three floors on my shoulder. I would ride the few yards along the corridor, and, once in the filing room, do a few quick tight laps round the big filing table before getting down to work.

Even such an eccentric as that, and a clumsy and hot-tempered one, too, was encouraged, trusted and drawn out by his colleagues and above all by his chiefs. Here, too, was a place of standards to which one could respond, though it was never codified as Christ's Hospital principles are in the noble words of the leaving service in chapel. Where much is expected, much is at least more likely to be given.

I owe a lot to those men I worked with or under in the nineteen twenties, Dawson Miller and his partner George Henry Vos; Victor Lofts with whom I shared the filing room; Jimmy Butlin, the solidly built clerk, eventually chief accountant and company secretary, who played Saturday football for Wealdstone in the Athenian League; Reggie Meyer, stocky veteran of the trenches in the First World War, who often joked his way out of self-contrived trouble; and Eddie Powley, another Saturday amateur league footballer from Leyton, tall, graceful, and athletic until he died at sixty or so.

Miller's was quite as much a school to me as Christ's Hospital, and almost the university I never went to. There, it was taken for granted that you felt yourself one of the team, and that if something needed doing, it would be done without discussion. Pay was low, but so it was everywhere then. Overtime pay was unheard of. If you worked after 6.30 p.m., you got half-a-crown 'tea money' to get something to eat on the way home. But the little community had the virtues of the small unit without many of its vices; the personal touch was there, the flexibility, and in our case also the family control. It's hard to describe. It was so much a matter of feeling, not of rules or logic.

The working conditions were grubby then. Office equipment was doled out parsimoniously. Victor Lofts and I only got authority to order new box files by staging a carefully arranged stack of broken and split examples which needed replacing. Towards the end of the month, lunch would be bought from a shop in Leadenhall Market where you could get a chunk of French bread for one (old) penny, a slap of butter for another penny, and a 'mini' packet of St Ivel cream cheese for twopence. Very satisfying. But it was a gay life. A couple of apples or a bag of hot chestnuts off a barrow were luxury to Victor and me.

All this, however, impinges also on the biggest way in which my work educated me. This was in knowledge of the intricate network which makes up human society. This could justify a book, or a series of books. It justifies at least a separate chapter.

8

The Cement of Society

Throughout my working life, I was learning day by day about human relationships, of the link-up between person and person, this organization and that, all the things which hold society together and make it effective. Much of it I explored doing my job. Much else I explored in outside activities. So, of course, does everyone.

Perhaps I have been extra lucky in both fields, work and leisure, for the reasons I explained in Chapter 1. Work took me to twenty-six other countries, and to some of them many times. My touch with Moral Re-Armament brought me into contact with many strata of society which I might never have penetrated otherwise.

The first people I met when I started the job were of course the people in the firm itself. In that small community there was little class distinction, except as between principals and staff. There were no gradations of management, except for the chief clerk, and of course no trade unions, nor any formal method of dealing between the 'bosses' and the 'workers'. You had to find out for yourself who did what, who had any right to order you around, and so forth. Some tried to order me around who had no right to, and some who had the right asked instead of ordering.

I believe, however, this rather vague situation is not uncommon in factories and other places which are supposed to be thoroughly organized. I heard an expert from the Industrial Society speak at a dinner for people in industry on the need for what they call in the fighting services a 'chain of command'. The expert had gone round parts of several factories, asking people, 'Who is your immediate boss?' Most of them did not know. One worker said : 'He is,' pointing to a man doing identical work. Another said : 'She is,' pointing to a shop steward.

I soon found that even a small business like ours did not work without some giving and some taking orders. It might be necessary for the man at the bottom (which at first was me) to go and ask for the order to be given, as it were, but there had to be some sort of system of decision and authority. Perhaps ideally one could dispense with anyone telling anyone else what to do, but we are not ideal subjects for the experiment.

On the other hand, there is a strong if not an unanswerable case for the maximum possible participation of everyone in decision-making, and the maximum of courtesy in both giving and receiving instructions. In general, my seniors were very good in explaining and in answering my questions; and when later I got confidence enough to make suggestions, these were given real consideration.

I found, too, that if I really wanted to take responsibility in and for the business, this was welcomed.

There is a great deal of chat nowadays about worker participation. Now that Britain has joined the European Economic Community, we must in a short time comply with the European laws which give workers a voice in the management of a business. In principle, this is an excellent thing. In practice, I am told by friends in Germany, where there are laws about it, that it can be either good or bad. It may turn out a complete waste of time.

I am not at all sure that some of those who call for 'worker-directors' are not simply doing it to further that out-of-date conception, the class war. What is the point of taking a good craftsman off his work, and sitting him down at a board-room table to consider matters he does not understand? Or of doing the same thing to a good full-time union official?

However, I am completely in favour of every worker having a clear road to the top, if he wants to follow it and is able to do so. Some dockers once asked John Houlder, chairman of Houlder Line, if he would be willing to have a docker on his board of directors. 'I'd be glad to,' he was reported as replying, 'if he was the right man for the job.' I know many men at the heads of businesses of different types who started at the bottom. I even know one who started on the factory floor, rose to be a director, and is now back on the factory floor again; but I don't think that proves anything!

I'm also totally in favour of maximum consultation at and with all levels in an undertaking. It is a difficult thing to do. The bigger our firm has got, the harder it has been to keep in touch with all sections of opinion, and to get the fertilization of ideas moving round and up and down. What it must be like in gigantic corporations like British Leyland or British Steel is difficult to imagine. Yet it is an essential requirement. It's much more than a house magazine (good though it may be) or a suggestion box. Suggestion boxes rather tend, I believe, to have a hole in the bottom and a waste-paper bin underneath.

Essentially, consultation is a human issue, and has to be done by means of small interlocking groups. And above all, the will to encourage it must be there.

In one of our better shipyards at the time I write, the chairman presides at board meetings; but apart from that he considers his main task is to sit at his desk with his door permanently open to anyone. Sometimes, for a change, he walks round the whole place, greeting people. The managing director manages the business.

Some thirty years ago I was taken over a Renold factory in Wales, making chains and sprockets and such. The management had found that a barrier had developed between the staff working on the machines and those in the office. One step they took was to replace the entire end wall of the offices by plate glass, so that each section of the factory could see clearly what went on in the other. It definitely had a uniting effect, they said.

As the years passed, much more of my own working time was spent in touch with people outside the office, especially in the world of ships. This world is complex in the extreme. One great section of such people, the experts we consult, has been introduced already in Chapter 2.

The group closest and most important to us was of course the shipowners and their staffs. They are a kaleidoscopic lot, of all shapes, sizes, nationalities and characteristics. In some countries, where government is authoritarian in one way or another, they are bureaucrats. In some, they are entrepreneurs, independent to the extent of eccentricity, daring or in other ways highly personal in their approach to life.

You can go into one office and find that the men who run it are a happy band of friends, joking and treating business as if it were a game of football. In another you will sit in embarrassment while the Big Boss tongue-lashes a senior manager, even in front of you, a visitor.

Some offices are luxurious and glossy, some cramped and dusty; but it is wise to suspend judgement as to which of the businesses are more efficient, and which are the more amply financed. Sometimes appearances are very deceptive.

Today, a few hours before I write these words, I was walking down St Mary Axe once again. On the steps of the Baltic Exchange, that world market of shipping, a man was standing. I nearly walked past, for it must be ten years since I saw him. I stopped, and went back. He was standing quietly on the bottom step, hands in pockets, for the wind was cold, his black soft hat pulled forward a little, and little expression on his tanned face, with its almost eagle-like nose. It was Panaghis Lykiardopulo, whose family firm has had its London office in that building for well over fifty years. How long they have been shipowners, I have no idea. It could be centuries. His father was one of the most respected men in the Greek Shipowners' Association in Athens; and when he finally resigned from its governing committee, it was because, he said, at ninety years he was getting a little old for committee work.

We shook hands warmly. It was as natural as if we had parted the week before. He said he had had a bad couple of years, with illness in the family ending in a sad bereavement. His voice was soft. I have never known him raise it, nor ever had him greet me or discuss anything except with grave and perfect courtesy. I asked after his son, once a big broad-shouldered athlete at Charterhouse, who sometimes seems rather English, but is also one hundred per cent Greek. 'He is upstairs,' said the father, gesturing upwards with his shoulders. It suggested, somehow, that all was well. I went on my way, feeling the better for the short encounter.

Behind him, in that building faced with brown marble, was his family firm. And that meant a long history, from caiques and sailing ships to modern tankers and bulk carriers. It meant a time when half a dozen small shipowners—'clients', the Greeks call them—also struggled or prospered in the Lykiardopulo shadow.

It meant boom times and hungry times, and ships manned with hardy islanders roving all the Seven Seas, with almost every kind of cargo. It meant accidents, problems and disputes. On one of the biggest of the disputes, I had worked for three or four years alongside Fotis Lykiardopulo, the son, until it was settled in 1963.

For over half a century our two firms have been linked. We have helped them, but in many ways they have helped us. Both Panaghis and Fotis have served on boards of directors of the mutual insurance association or 'clubs' which we managed, and their advice has often been above price.

The surroundings of one of our other very long-term shipowner friends could hardly be more different—Shell Tankers, somewhere in that great tower block of the Shell group on the South Bank of the Thames, near Waterloo Station and the Royal Festival Hall. It is of course only one aspect of the great oil operation, which includes production, refining, an extensive chemical industry, and transport by other methods as well as ships. The 'shipowners' part is just a few floors in the tower which was said, after it was opened, to hold 9,000 workers and already to be insufficient for the expanding business. When I started delivering letters round the City in 1924, the Shell group was in St Helen's Court, a rambling complex of offices spanning Great St Helen's and Crosby Square, and I mainly remember them for having the haughtiest commissionaires of all those to whom I handed letters. But perhaps that was because I tried to use their office as a short cut.

As far back as the fifties and sixties, Shell owned several million tons of tank ships, and had millions more chartered from independent owners. Two things in particular I find remarkable in them. One is that they still name their ships after sea shells, which was the commodity which the company sold in the nineteenth century (to ornament photograph frames, for example) before they ever dipped into oil. The other is that such a vast organization, operating in scores of countries, has been able to keep the personal touch with people, at least as far as my contacts showed over the years.

The senior man we dealt with there in connection with chartered ships for a number of years was A. J. Roper. John Roper and I did not always agree, and in fact one matter over which we differed was fought through the courts right up to the House of

Lords. But he was an agreeable man to deal with, and very straightforward.

One of the occasions when I visited him was to accompany the young manager of a shipowning company who had been arguing a point by correspondence. Shell had chartered a new tanker from that company for a period of five years. Since she was a steamer and not a motorship, she had to be taken out of service every year or so for routine cleaning of the boilers, to maintain her efficiency. There was a provision in the charter-party that Shell would not pay hire during this operation. An argument developed as to exactly what the words meant, and the result of this in terms of money. The cleaning took only a day or so, so not much money was involved, some hundreds of pounds, perhaps.

I felt that the issue was worth arguing, but not one for which one had to be willing to die on the barricades, as it were. Yet when we sat down in Roper's office, and it became fairly clear that he was not prepared to give way, the young manager went on and on, and got more and more heated in his arguments. The hotter things got on our side of the table, the colder they got on the other. Eventually, I could stand it no longer, and had to say to my friend, even in front of Roper, 'Hold on a minute. Mr Roper clearly thinks you are being unreasonable. You have just started a five-year relationship with his company which gives profitable employment for a big ship. Do you want to start with a dispute which could colour all your dealings together for the next five years?' The tension eased instantly. Roper smiled. The impetuous young man decided to yield the point, and I believe that they worked well together thereafter.

I could tell a thousand yarns about shipowners, and it is fascinating just to let memory range over some of the offices I have walked into. There is that of United States Lines, in the block which has perhaps the most striking address of any in the world, Number One, Broadway, New York City. There was the little upstairs office, partitioned off from a spicy-smelling warehouse in Madurai, the inland city in South India which boasts some of the most spectacular Hindu temples anywhere. A couple of ships were run from there. Others, trading to the Andaman Islands, were managed from an office in a side-alley off a narrow Calcutta street, an alley I ducked into rather quickly as a chanting crowd waving red flags surged into the street in one of the political demonstrations which are not uncommon in that volatile city.

There was the Chinese shipowning firm in Singapore in whose waiting-room there was a ship model several feet long, her hull, masts, sails, and rigging painstakingly pieced together from tooth-picks. I was hoping to get their business. I had no luck with that; but they took us out for a splendid authentically Chinese meal at a fine restaurant, far from the tourist area. My wife, in her first attempt at using chopsticks, brought applause from our hosts by getting a pigeon's egg, floating in a bowl of soup, up and into her mouth at one go. At the end of the meal, the waiters brought a great dish of luscious sliced oranges. 'I'm sorry about this,' explained the host, 'but a tradition has grown up in this restaurant that the waiters get the money for the oranges as well as the tip, so everyone gets oranges whether they order them or not.' The firm was at an interesting stage. They had moved out of junks into coasting motor vessels, of which they owned several scores. Now they were buying bigger and longer-distance ships, and when we were there they were starting a regular liner service to Australia.

And in Genoa I called on yet another man, totally different from any other. E. N. Vintiadis was a ship's agent as well as a shipowner. His office was in a sixteenth-century palazzo in an old part of the city. You walked through a discoloured stone arch into the central courtyard, which had been glassed over several storeys above. In the courtyard had been installed a creaking, wobbling lift. Mr Vintiadis was a Greek living in Italy. His room seemed full of people (though I don't think there were more than eight or ten), papers, ash-trays, and coffee cups. Everyone talked at once, in English, Greek and Italian, and he seemed to take part in all the conversations, whilst welcoming me warmly, too, and discussing whatever we had to discuss. Behind his chair was a big wide-open safe. At one point, he reached into it and pulled out a bundle of notes which seemed to be as big as my head, and a thick wad of it was counted out for a captain who had come in and needed some cash.

In Split, in Yugoslavia, the shipowning concern ('enterprise' is their word for a company) was housed in a new office block, over-looking the beautiful curve of the bay. It was not large by London standards, but smart and efficient. The atmosphere was something between a British or Scandinavian company, and a government department. An effective contrast to its modernity was that only a short walk away stood the vast palace, almost a town in itself, built by the Roman emperor Diocletian in the fourth century A.D.

Perhaps I may insert here a story I was told in Beograd. An alligator escaped from the zoo. Looking for a suitable home in the warm basement of a big office building, he found in the boiler room another alligator. Except for one thing, it was a grand place, the newcomer was told. There was plenty to eat. All you had to do was to slip up the back stairs after lunch, when all was quiet, and snap up one of the senior officials. No one even noticed he had gone. 'What was the snag?' asked the newcomer. 'I did a very silly thing yesterday,' said the old resident, 'I gobbled up the little girl who makes the coffee, and now they are searching the whole building.' You have heard that story before? I am not surprised. But when I first heard it, fifteen years ago, it was piquant to have it told by a Communist in a Communist capital city.

My theme seems to have escaped, too. This chapter was to have been about how all kinds of people and organizations affect each other. But Mr Vintiadis' office was one example. In that smoke-filled room many different threads were knotted together. The Baltic Exchange, of which I am proud to be a life member, is another and a bigger example. On its spacious floor, amongst shipowners, merchants, and a score of different kinds of brokers, you can buy yourself a ship, find employment for her, arrange for her crew to be flown out to her, buy the oil for her fuel, arrange for her repairs, and eventually sell her again. A man can say 'yes' to another on the Baltic, before any documents are exchanged, and know that they have made a contract, maybe for a million pounds, or ten million.

All kinds of businesses are part of the web, and all kinds of institutions. I wonder what proportion of the people who live in the United Kingdom has heard of the National Maritime Board. A small proportion, I would guess. It is a joint organization of the shipowners, the seamen's and officers' unions, and the captains' professional body. For many years they have progressively and peacefully worked together to regulate the wages and working conditions of seafarers. The changes have been slow and undramatic, but their aggregate result is astonishing. The measure of agreement can be judged by the fact that the seamen's strike of 1966 was the first official strike in the industry for fifty-five years.

The interest we as insurers have had in their work is indirect. It is we who have paid for many of the benefits the Board have agreed on, year by year. For example, when the National Maritime Board decided that some compensation should be paid if crew members had their clothes and effects destroyed by shipwreck, fire, or flooding of their cabins, my firm and the other P. and I. clubs immediately decided to widen their insurance cover, so as to refund the cost to the shipowners. Most countries now have similar arrangements for their ships, either by law or by agreement.

One little sidelight on the progress made in improving seamen's conditions came when I was invited to the trials of a new-built ship off the Tyne. I went all over her in company with two fellow-guests, Hugh Hogarth, the Glasgow shipowner, and Allan Manson, then assistant general secretary of the National Union of Seamen. We saw the individual cabins for each man of the crew, the seamen's mess-room, and other facilities, and Mr Manson's wry comment was : 'I went to sea in the wrong ships at the wrong time.'

Ships' agents are another very essential part of the world network of the industry. Wherever a ship may call, there needs to be someone ashore who can organize fresh provisions, take charge of a sick or injured man, and do any or all of a score of jobs which the captain, however able, has no time for. Some are such firms as Phs. van Ommeren in Rotterdam (and many other places), with their tower building by the riverside. When I was last there, they had still not gained government permission to use the helicopter platform they had hopefully built on the roof when the block was constructed, but the fact that they had one at least shows their forward-looking approach to business. They of course are shipowners, too, barge-owners, container operators, and many other things; but agency for visiting ships is a big part of their business, and the handsome room just inside the entrance is 'the captains' room'. They take pleasure in showing business visitors the port from their motor-launch; and when they did this for us, my wife was very touched by their courtesy in breaking out our country's flag from the little mast on the launch as we stepped aboard.

Ships' agents, like shipowners, come in all shapes and sizes. Some specialize in that work. Some combine it with various other activities. The biggest ships' agents in Cyprus also run a travel agency, and import refrigerators and motor vehicles. Our P. and I. club's correspondents in Japan, Dodwell & Co. Ltd., consider themselves primarily, I think, import and export merchants, but their ships' agents department, when I was there in 1962, seemed to me to contain a couple of hundred people in a huge room, all of them speaking busily into telephones. At the entrance was a board with the names of all the ships then in port, or expected, a long list, with many names which I recognized at a glance.

In a port in Sicily, however, one office I visited seemed to consist of one man only, with a woman secretary. He was immensely energetic, but I left wondering what happened if, say, he caught influenza when a ship was due.

When returning from India by ship, my wife and I had a few hours ashore in Gibraltar, and paid a courtesy call on the club's representative there. They were also ships' agents, and travel agents, in two or three rooms. The manager almost fell on my neck in welcome. 'I'm so glad to see you,' he said, 'I've got a problem which seems to have no possible answer.' A ship insured with us and owned in Finland had called briefly at Gibraltar, and discharged into hospital a seaman suffering from a serious mental illness. Unfortunately he spoke nothing but Finnish. No one could be found in the whole of Gibraltar who spoke Finnish, so the hospital could not even diagnose his condition, let alone treat it. 'Very simple,' I said. 'Cable to the club in London, and ask them to get the shipowners to send out a Finnish doctor, to take him back to hospital in Finland.' He punched his own forehead shamefacedly, but of course it was a unique situation to him. With all the cross-currents of world-wide events which flow across our desks in London, it was much easier for me than for him to get perspective on such a thing.

We had in previous years had equally unusual situations. One was a British seaman discharged in North Africa, whose mental trouble was of a violent nature. A doctor had to be sent out to bring him home in a strait-jacket. Another was a Greek wireless operator discharged in Liverpool suffering from leprosy. A small isolation hospital had to be specially opened to receive him. When we tried to get him back to Greece we found that from exaggerated fear of contagion, no airline, railway, or shipping company would carry him. We chartered a small aircraft and flew him back to Greece with a young doctor and one of our staff to look after him. In Greece there are still (or were at that time) leper hospitals.

At that time, it was quite an event in the shipping world to charter an aircraft. Today, it is routine. Large planes are often used to replace crews whose period of employment has been completed, to bring home shipwrecked crews, and to take spare parts out to ships whose machinery has broken down. If delay to a ship means a loss of a thousand pounds a day (and it could be much more) simple arithmetic encourages the quickest possible means of getting her moving again.

It can even be worthwhile to use the air to avoid a ship putting into port, which is itself a costly business. Many of the large tankers carrying oil from the Middle East are regularly supplied off the Cape of Good Hope by helicopter with mails, fresh foodstuffs and other supplies. Sick or injured men are taken off by the same means all over the world. When there was a bomb hoax on the *Queen Elizabeth 2*, the whole world watched on television the bomb disposal experts boarding her by helicopter. Every week surveyors and other experts arrive or depart from some ship or other for more prosaic reasons. Even pilots arrive and depart in this way sometimes, instead of by the traditional rope ladder.

All kinds of other auxiliary people have their key parts in operating ships, divers to inspect underwater, barges to bring oil and water alongside, and other barges to take away contaminated ballast and waste, repairers for everything from heavy plating to electronic gear, advisers, experts, investigators. Every shipowner of any size has on his staff superintendents to keep the ships in good condition and fully equipped. And so it goes on.

One way or another, I had contact with people in most of these fields, as well as the bankers, insurers and brokers who were always at hand when needed. I relished it all, and also the different circles to which my touch with Moral Re-Armament was the key. If you know and associate with people whose basic idea is to help the world to change for the better through change in people, it does expose you to a variety of adventures.

Not long after I first met these ideas in 1933, a group of my new friends began working together in East London. It was a grim time. Trade was so bad that many shops were boarded up. Mosley's 'black shirts' were holding marches, and fighting hand to hand in the streets with bands of the extreme left. Bitterness and suspicion were normal. I used to go down in the evenings to meet with the others, some of them also in jobs, some who had decided to work full-time without pay. We would go 'on the knocker' from house to house, to get to know people, arrange meetings in schools, halls, and the upper rooms of pubs, and take any means of encouraging better ideas. It was all very experimental, but it certainly had a definite and permanent effect on some people, and there were those who said the effect was widespread.

I found it a long journey home to South London some of those nights, and after talking it over with my wife, I offered to stay down in East London for a month, going in to the office each day, but free to help with the other work in the evenings. Someone or another managed to fix me a room in the Isle of Dogs, near the docks. My host was an old widower, living alone on a tiny pension in a little terrace house, two rooms up and two down. When I arrived, he took me up to the back bedroom, and explained the sanitary arrangements in the cockney fashion : 'The whatsit is down the yard, but I've put the fireman's 'elmet under the bed.' I paid him something, all I could afford, but he insisted on cooking me a hot breakfast every morning before I went to work.

I met some colourful characters down there, an engine-driver, a window-cleaner, and a number of unemployed. One man, in the course of a chat, pulled up his jersey to show me an eight-inch scar across his stomach. Someone had stuck a knife into him during a little misunderstanding at the races.

There was Alderman Freddie Welch, deputy mayor of one of the East London boroughs. In his youth he had been a professional footballer, and played for Sunderland. He was still neat and erect, and although his face was lined, his hair was raven black, greased straight back. He had been a Labour man of the old school, good at heart, but the bitterness showed through. He was deeply changed by the M.R.A. ideas, and became reconciled with enemies he had made in his own party. This also had an effect on the Conservative minority on the council. The big annual debate was always on the fixing of the rate, to cover the cost of all the services provided by the council. This debate was a noisy affair. It always went on for several hours, and every device of opposition was employed. When the date for a rate-fixing next came round after Freddie's initial change, the leader of the Labour majority group explained their plans, and formally proposed adoption of them. Before anyone else could speak, the leader of the Conservatives rose, announced that his party agreed, and seconded the motion. End of debate.

One thing we found out was that some of the unemployed, with nothing else to do, had somehow acquired some football equipment, and played regularly twice a week. Someone issued a challenge, and a scratch team was raised of M.R.A. men. We met on the old Clapton Orient ground, the 'Spotted Dog', and I got half a day off work to play at right back. It was an extraordinary occasion. I, for example, brought up on Rugby football not Association, kept on finding myself trying to defend the whole goal line, instead of the goal. Our goalkeeper, who had never played this type of football before, came out to ask me : 'Am I allowed to catch the ball, or do I have to stop it, and then pick it up?' But for our centre half, a curate who had (long before) played for Crystal Palace as an amateur, the score would have been much worse than 8-1 against us.

It was a battle of ideas, too, for a good band of their supporters turned up. One had a bugle, and some of them sang a chorus of 'The Red Flag' every time their team scored. But we all went over to the 'Spotted Dog' public house for tea afterwards, including, I think, the referee, a famous England international named Jimmy Ruffell, who kept a greengrocer's shop nearby. There was a feeling that, although they won the match, we had done something towards winning the men.

I ached for days afterwards. But I still laugh over our efforts that afternoon with our goalkeeper Edward Evans, now an internationally-known farmer and recently High Sheriff of Herefordshire. Rather naturally he remembers vividly the one shot by their centre-forward Morgan which he brilliantly saved, rather than the ones he let through. Our centre-forward Michael Sitwell was, alas, killed on the Normandy beaches in 1944.

Not all the people I met in this way were in East London, or unemployed. One is now a well-known bishop. During the war, when I was helping to keep Moral Re-Armament's London head-quarters running, I often used to wash up the communal breakfast things with Lord Addington, a Conservative peer, and George Light, chairman of the National Trade Union Club. Another I got to know at that time was Group-Captain Patrick Foss, who had commanded the bombers in Malta, and was then in a top job in Transport Command at the Air Ministry; and yet another was Arthur Baker, chief of the parliamentary staff of *The Times* and author of *The House is Sitting*. None of these was likely to frequent St Mary Axe.

A few years after the war, when the coal mines had been nationalized, I called with a friend to see the secretary of a branch of the National Union of Mineworkers in Staffordshire. A shift had just finished. Whether there were pithead baths in those days and at that pit, I do not know; but if there were, the men had decided that a mug of tea and a bite was an earlier priority, for the canteen was crammed with blackened faces and working clothes. We spoke to one of them, who shouted : 'Aaron !' and shouldered off through the crowd. The secretary emerged, as black as the rest, recognized us and laughed. 'He said there were two chaps,' he explained, 'I asked him what sort of chaps, and he said they looked like National Coal Board chaps.'

Aaron Colclough was one of several miners' leaders whom I met at that period. In 1946/47 large groups of miners from most of the major coalfields in England, Scotland and Wales came to London for conferences and to see at the Westminster Theatre an industrial drama called *The Forgotten Factor*. Written by Alan Thornhill, a former Oxford don, it shows how change can come to a deadlocked industrial situation. I say 'shows' rather than showed, as the play is still being staged in various languages all over the world, and literally millions have seen it. I last heard of it being done near Poona in India, the language being Marathi.

This was the time when Ernie Bevin, Foreign Minister in Attlee's government, said : 'Give me coal, and I will give you a foreign policy.' In industry after the war, nearly everything and everybody was worn out. Nationalization of the mines did not solve everything instantly, as some dreamers hoped. Other European countries were even worse off, and the Atlantic was crowded with ships bringing coal to Europe. Production in the British mines made a fine recovery. Many, including some who are now high in the union, give part of the credit for that to the men who found new ideas in *The Forgotten Factor*. One phrase especially became almost a catchword—'Not who's right, but what's right'. And men in Yorkshire still talk of the manager they called 'the pocket battleship', and of how he learnt co-operation with the men after years of industrial warfare.

My wife and I were one of a score of business and professional couples who formed a trust and bought the Westminster Theatre, so that it could be available when needed to present plays sponsored by Moral Re-Armament. Experiments in Britain and the U.S.A. had already shown the effectiveness of the theatre for putting across ideas. It is hardly a novel notion. One has only to think of the ancient Greek dramatists and the medieval mystery plays, and in more modern times Shaw, Priestley, Brecht and Sartre.

The operation had its bizarre aspects. I was probably the junior of the twenty. My pay was about a fifth of what a coalface miner earns today. But none of us was wealthy, and Lionel Exton, the man who signed the cheque for the deposit, had to overdraw his account to do so. He offered his bank manager his house as security, but was told that his name was enough.

Then, speed and discretion were important, if we were not to have some theatre tycoon overbidding us. So we had to raise a sum running into six figures in sterling in six weeks, without publicity other than word of mouth. However, hundreds of people responded, many of them men and women of the fighting services who gave the gratuities paid to them on their discharge that year. I can remember one evening when four or five of us met. Time was getting short, and the flow of money seemed to have dried up. Someone suggested prayer, and we knelt down together in that basement room. As we stood up again, the telephone rang. It was a lady in Lancashire, who said that she had been entrusted several years before with some money to be used for a good purpose connected with the theatre. This scheme, she felt, was what she had been waiting for. It was, if I remember rightly, £7,000, and about the largest single gift we received. Also, the small gifts began to arrive again, and the entire sum needed was put together before the deadline.

Another thing was that none of us had any idea how to run a theatre. I hasten to say that I still don't know. But one of the men who did take it on, after experience only in a firm which made barrels, is now a respected figure in the Society of West End Theatre Managers.

In the years since, many fine productions have seen the light first there, some sponsored by the theatre itself and by Moral Re-Armament, some by other managements to which it has been let. Although I have not had the joys and sorrows of management, I have had the privilege of being chairman for some years of the Friends of the Westminster Theatre. Through this I have sometimes met professional actors, directors of plays, dramatists and others, who also (like the miners) do not frequent St Mary Axe. And I have been able to see for myself that the venture has effectively achieved what we planned for in 1946.

Some are convinced that its influence is far wider, in two ways. At one time, it was difficult to find plays in London to which people with principles (diplomats from Muslim countries, for example) could comfortably take their families. The Westminster has shown that plays which respect principles can consistently be shown, and can entertain. Its original children's pantomime, *Give a Dog a Bone*, had eleven successive and successful Christmas seasons. Furthermore, a number of these productions have also been presented in scores of countries overseas, and filmed in many languages for cinema and television. One Commonwealth prime minister uses these films regularly to entertain official guests. Audiences altogether total many millions.

What has all this to do with the shipping industry? As regards the theatre, a seaman ashore looks for entertainment. So does a business visitor from abroad after a hard's day's work. And they should have the chance of the right kind of entertainment.

On the broader issues, ships will only be used to the full by countries which are busy, united, and friendly to each other. Anything, therefore, which helps industry to function efficiently

G

and makes for a stable society is (in one sense) the business of any-one whose life is lived in the shipping industry.

In recent years, we have had the 'theatre of the absurd', the 'theatre of cruelty', and theatre deeply affected by left-wing revo-lutionary thinking, as well as frequent repetitions of two limited aspects of human life, sexual indulgence and the 'kitchen sink'. It is against this background that one really needs to assess the signi-ficance of plays which, in very varied ways, express a theatre of humanity and hope.

9

Management is a Problem

Everyone criticizes management. If a company collapses in England or France, some enthusiasts for workers' control call for the workers to occupy the factory or offices, and maybe for the government to supply capital so that the workers can run the business themselves.

Many politicians and many civil servants think they should tell the management of industry and commerce what to do. An extreme case of this, according to what I was told by a man who should know, has been the British Steel Corporation, where ministers (both Labour and Conservative), civil servants, and the men who run the Corporation have fought a three-sided battle as to who should decide policy. Prices, manning, and the maintenance of obsolete plants have all been treated as political issues.

On countless occasions, when trouble has hit an industry (nationalized or private) or a company, union officials have blamed the management.

Sometimes the critics have been right. Often, they have not. But in my experience the most strenuous critics of management have (most commonly) been the managers themselves.

As for those who think anyone can exercise what control is necessary, I wish they could have been with me on my first long visit to Yugoslavia after the Second World War. We saw nearly all the top people in shipowning and insurance. Almost the whole of the previous management echelon had been disposed of by war and revolution. They were dead or in exile. It was said that Ante Topic, one of the shipowners, had been offered by President Tito the post of Minister of Merchant Marine, with full powers, but he preferred running a few ships from London for his own account, to going back.

The authorities had found it vital to assemble a new management cadre at once, and scraped round everywhere for them. Some had gone straight from school to join the partisans in the mountains. Their only experience was as guerrilla leaders. Several had been captains of merchant ships; one had been Tito's interpreter in the mountains; another a lawyer. Several young women had responsible posts.

The point was that, to get the country's economy working, there had to be managers, with authority to make decisions, and supplied with capital (in this case from the state or local authorities) to pay for what needed to be done.

Naturally, I know most about my own firm. Here, I have had the chance to observe management at work from below, from alongside, and to some extent from a higher position in the hierarchy. We have had outside criticism at times, from rivals, from the shipowners whose interests we are employed to serve, and from the supervising boards. Sometimes it has been justified. But the most violent and penetrating attacks on our weaknesses have mostly been amongst ourselves. Occasionally they have caused deep, if temporary, divisions.

I remember a particular incident where one of us had taken a course of action, of which several others violently disapproved. The man concerned had some support, and yet others (who perhaps had not considered it thoroughly) said it did not matter greatly one way or the other. For some, however, it was a question of far-reaching principle, and their feelings were very strong. A showdown was to take place at a certain meeting; and the day before this the man demanding the showdown asked me to support him. I agreed. But when the item on the agenda was called, the one under attack immediately said that he had now discussed the point fully with his critic. He saw that he had been wrong, and was taking steps to put matters right.

Another time, I myself was accused in a management meeting of a breach of business ethics. I disagreed, but others, including my own senior partner, said that I had, intentionally or not, broken an agreement, and I had to swallow the rebuke.

I know of similar situations in other firms. Sometimes, it has made me wonder if you cannot have a dynamic and progressive undertaking without internal friction, without indeed almost as many and constant explosions as a diesel engine! The great thing is not whether you agree together, but what you do about it when you disagree. Our business is one of a number I have known well where the group who run it are not naturally compatible people. They have very diverse talents. It was by no means unknown for me, for example, to be on some issue a minority of one. Could I accept that position with grace, and continue to work for what I felt right on every issue, or would resentment take over, and immobilize me to some degree?

These things may not seem vital to the quality of management, but they are. More losses result from board-room feuds than from ineptitude; and more important still is the positive effect of a team which can disagree and still fight on together to achieve their common task. In such an atmosphere, inept operators have no place. They fall by the wayside; though, if the vigorous characters are humane and creative, they may find quiet places where the casualties can recover, and still make a contribution.

The biggest factor in management is, after all, the management of people. Ideas, techniques and money are important; but without men and women who can and will work together, the other things produce nothing.

Perhaps, later in this book, I will try to consider the question which a friendly rival in another firm asked me once when we and our wives spent an evening together: 'Tell me, how do you deal with difficult people?' I never answered him, because at that moment the theatre's curtain went up for the second act, and somehow we never got back to the question, but it is one to which any good manager must ponder the answer daily. I remember an occasion when a friend and (in one sense) a colleague of mine was fuming over the way another man had behaved. He tried to get a more senior person to put pressure on the culprit, or perhaps I should say the person my friend considered to be the culprit. All the senior would say, however, was: 'I made up my mind long ago that I was going to work with difficult people for the rest of my life. You might consider doing the same.' The response had a curious effect. It not only made my friend easier for everyone to work with from then on, but it also made him realize that he had helped to cause the original difficulty. When he admitted this, the 'culprit' became markedly different.

Just three years after I finished my forty-eight years in St Mary Axe, and made a clean break with the job I had been doing all that time, I had a surprising telephone call. It conveyed a unanimous invitation to go back on a part-time basis, say one day a week, to reinstate a management training programme in the firm.

It was put in a very charming and indeed flattering way. In the last eight years before retirement, I had been responsible for our first systematic training of those promoted to or engaged for junior management posts. The complicated nature of the business, and its big expansion, meant that some new people needed training each year. I knew that, after I retired, younger partners had taken on the training, but it had not wholly been a success. This was partly due to other pressures on the partners, but perhaps was also because no one had had quite the same conviction about the task that I had had. Whatever the reasons, it was felt that the people recently recruited noticeably lacked some things which were common to those I had trained earlier.

My feelings about it were extremely mixed. I felt flattered, of course. It is pleasant to feel you are needed. It would be very enjoyable to match my wits again with a bunch of eager and talented people forty years younger than I. I felt a great obligation to the firm which had meant so much to my life, and had as far as possible kept warm my friendships with many there. On the other hand, I had become accustomed to living without the pressure of regular hours. I had many useful activities. Also, my knowledge of the fast-changing world of ships and insurance was already three years out of date, and I felt appreciably slower in mind and body.

We decided to consult other friends who believed, as we did, that guidance might be had from the Spirit, to whatever extent it was needed. A telephone call produced an invitation to lunch with a father, mother and daughter. I spelt out all the facts, and we sat together quietly for a while, with paper and pencils for any thoughts worth recording. All of us were positive about the plan (for me, there seemed many pointers) but the most arresting thought was contributed by our host : 'If you accept, do it for one year only, during which you must prepare your successor.'

Call it common sense, if you like, but this immediately clarified the picture. It was essential to secure the future position. I went back to the partners with these ideas. They received them cordially, and said they had already begun to think the same way. As early as possible, some experienced person must be discovered or chosen who would start working with me. Before the year was up, I ought rather to be assisting him, sitting in his shadow, as it were, while he did it.

On my past experience, I had found that training was best done as a part-time job by a man deeply involved in running the business, who makes a decision that, come what may, he will set aside the time for a proper training programme. It is no light task.

How do you train people for management? Probably the ideal system is different for every different kind of business. I have described my own original system in print elsewhere. Now it had to be changed. Instead of a busy executive, giving part of every day to training, I had become a consultant giving one day a week.

I went over the manual I had prepared for the original course, and found it good in parts, inadequate in others. I also felt myself inadequate on a number of the subjects covered.

The first task was to get to know the newcomers. There were eight, seven men and a woman, all in their twenties. All had had higher education, either at universities or for the Bar examinations (or both), or in one case, an ex-soldier, at Sandhurst. My first impression was that they were a group of high potential. This dealt with stage one, as it were, for the first thing to do is to select people of real management capability. It was apparent that the firm was still paying great attention to the selection process, and comments by one or two of the group confirmed this to me.

It is, incidentally, a process which needs a lot of hard work by the selectors, a real insight into people, and a willingness to back a hunch. I have done some work in this field, although another partner in the firm is the real specialist. It is amusing to look back on some of the interviews I participated in. One young man admitted to a knowledge of French, and the two senior partners (both bilingual) started to enquire closely, in French, into his views on certain gastronomic matters. He was a bit shaken, but plunged in and did well. (He is still doing well.) A master mariner who had left the sea came up for interview, and made such a good impression that we took him on, although we had no job in view for him at that time. He did well, too. On the other side of the balance sheet, one could put a very able young man who at Cambridge had chaired one of the chief political clubs. In most ways, he was excellent. Then he said : 'I hope in due course to stand for a seat in Parliament. I take it I would be given leave to pursue my political aims.' In some businesses this might be practicable, but we had to say, 'Not in this firm.'

In spite of the care we take, we have failures, of course. One man started off extremely well, then seemed to come to a full stop, and developed no further. I had grave doubts about another man, who seemed nice enough, but had no cutting edge, as far as I could see. My colleagues decided he should be tried out, and they proved to be right, and I wrong.

The bunch I was faced with on my return were varied in temperament and background, which showed that we were still keeping an open mind, and recruiting a mixture of promising types rather than applying a formula. A class of eight, however, was really very large. The ideal ratio for management training is one teacher, one pupil. To have up to four pupils at a time is quite good. They help and stimulate each other. Five is a bit much. Eight is rough on the instructor, and certainly not ideal for the pupils, the quieter of whom are tempted to lapse into silence and ignorance.

The problem was how, in a few months, to help them to operate effectively in a business which managed six mutual insurance associations, all different, dealt with shipowners of seventy different countries and with everything which could happen to a ship anywhere on the seas of the world. In a way, it was a crazy task, but I regard it as rather like the driving test. Your instructor does not try to teach you everything, but only enough to make you reasonably safe on the road, and to provide a basic pattern of behaviour. One reason why our British roads are less dangerous than in some countries is that the Ministry of Transport driving tests do impose a basic code on all new British drivers.

To begin with, I built up the course week by week, consulting the students themselves on what to do next. In the execution of it, I tried to do two things. One was to pictorialize and humanize the technical aspects. The other was to involve many other people in the presentation.

The first session dealt with the shipping industry. I did a very brief survey of its history; the sequence of expansion of maritime nations through fishing, then piracy, then trade, then colonization; the junks in the Far East trans-shipping on the Malabar coast into Arab dhows the luxuries demanded by the declining Roman Empire; caravels, galleons and clipper ships. Then a former ship-owner told how ships are run today, and what has to be organized by whom when a ship comes in : cargo handling, crew changes, drydocking and repairs, stores and fuel oil.

The next week we talked about ships of today. Three men holding deep-sea masters' certificates presented different aspects, showed plans and pictures, and answered questions. Then a Lloyd's insurance broker came to talk about marine insurance historically and today.

Many others in the firm contributed to the course. One of the secretaries ended her contribution with a vigorous plea that she and the other girls should be treated as people and colleagues, rather than just as women. She added pungent examples of how to do it and not to do it.

A partner, asked to speak about business relationships, began by saying that each one was a relationship of trust, built up on honesty. He went on to say that this was not merely not telling lies. It meant having the technical prowess to be sure that everything you did and said was precisely accurate, and backed by work of similar quality from your colleagues. As an example, he spoke of a firm of shipowners in the Far East who, on his first visit, propounded and argued nearly a hundred points, many quite trivial. He patiently dealt with all of them. Two or three visits later, any technical statement to which he committed himself was accepted without question.

I was gratified to hear, when I plunged for the second time into the sea of training, that the firm was doing even better than in my time. It had a larger share of the world market. Part of the success was attributed to the thirty-two people I had trained earlier, of whom two were already partners in the firm. However, I felt I had failed to make adequate provision for training after I left.

In all the above, I have said nothing about the various facilities for management training available outside our own office. This is because our work is so specialized and intricate that outside courses are of little use. There is now a wealth of such courses for those who need them. My own son, seeking further knowledge and ability, started at the age of forty a course with the Open University. My personal friends include lecturers on personnel relations at Coventry and management accounting in Essex. At one time I was very sceptical of the academic approach to these subjects, but I feel sure now that they do much valuable work.

Whatever the critics say, there is a lot of admiration overseas for the quality of British management and administration. It is vital that we aim to improve that quality in every possible way.

The first step in doing so is acceptance of the principle that management is a key function in a developed society, and is one of the three great partners which must work together in any substantial undertaking—capital, management and labour. They are not of their nature antagonists. In fact, they often overlap. Workers hold shares in their companies. Managers work alongside other workers. Dr Frank Buchman, who first used the phrase 'moral re-armament', spoke in one of his best-known statements of how, when rightly guided, 'capital and labour work together, like the fingers on the hand. Each man has a share in labour. Each man builds up the nation's capital'.

Management is the key to unity in industry. Those who fulfil this vital function need to be given recognition, and supported by all who are interested in a society which works.

10

The Profit Motive

To some, the profit motive is an abomination. To others, it is the true basis for an economy which works. The truth, surely, is somewhere in between.

I believe the profit motive exists in every one of us. It is part of the instinct of self-preservation, as basic as the sexual urge; and, like the sexual urge, it can work for good or ill. Each of our remote ancestors, as he cleared a patch of forest, fought off the wolves, or planted his first crops, exemplified the profit motive, as he sought for something better and more stable for himself and his family.

My own business surroundings were a curious blend of profit-making and non-profit-making. The mutual insurance associations we manage are non-profit-making bodies. They have no share capital, pay no dividends, and seek only to balance income with outgoings. The system has worked admirably for over a hundred years. The management firm, on the other hand, makes profits out of its work, sharing these between the partners. As the years went on, I became more convinced that the fact that we risked our incomes, but would be rewarded if our work was done really effectively, put an edge on the way we did the work. If your own interests are acutely at risk, it inspires maximum effort, and our interests as managers ran closely parallel with those of the associations. If they progressed, we prospered. If we flagged, their progress hesitated.

Furthermore, if we were efficient enough to make reasonable profits, we could afford to provide adequate pay and conditions for our staff. Our basic method is to pay everyone on a scale a little over the average for the type of work, with extra for those individuals who do well or take a special degree of responsibility. All salaries were, when I retired, reviewed twice yearly.

None of this is remarkable. The point is that without profits no commercially-run concern can exist. The employment of its workers depends on profits being made. Winston Churchill once said : 'It is a socialist idea that making profits is a vice; I consider the real vice is making losses.' I take his point, but what he calls a socialist idea is not supported by all socialists. In Yugoslavia, for example, every undertaking has to account to the Ministry of Finance. If there are no profits, the Ministry wants to know why. My wife asked a Yugoslav whether there was much crime there. 'Oh, yes !' was the reply. So she asked what type of crime worried the authorities most. The answer was emphatic : 'Bad business management.' Those who do not produce good results may not only lose their jobs. They may go to jail.

Profits do not merely mean employment. They are essential for the equipment of industry. For years critics of Britain, friendly or otherwise, have complained that capital investment in industry is too low. Essentially, this capital investment has to come out of profits. Those who attack the very idea of profit are also attacking the possibility of investing for expansion. I am not one who believes in continual expansion of everything. Heaven forbid. But there are still many important human needs unmet, on a very large scale. In these fields expansion is essential.

Most of us in fact would like to make a profit out of our activities. We want more than bare existence. A year or so after I got married, I had a small rise in salary. I was so excited that as I entered our kitchen/living-room at the top of 13 Helix Road, off Brixton Hill, I threw the small handful of notes which was my month's pay across the room to my wife as she stood at the stove. They fluttered everywhere. One fell in the frying pan. Out of this tiny increase in affluence I bought her a little rabbit in clear, polished Brazilian crystal. When, later, it was dropped and shattered, she wept.

Yet men and women are not prisoners of the profit motive. At one time, during the Second World War, there were 102 ship-owners working without salary at the Ministry of War Transport in London. The United States had its 'dollar a year' men, in the same way. The Commonwealth Development Finance Company was formed in London to help the less wealthy countries of the Commonwealth with new development projects. With government encouragement, private enterprise companies like Shell Petroleum, the P. & O. Line, Metal Box, Unilever and many others subscribed the ordinary capital, and quite deliberately went without any dividends for the first eleven years. The scheme might bring indirect advantages to the companies in due course, but it was a very remarkable conception of capitalist financing.

The day I wrote this paragraph, a man told me that, since his retirement from teaching, he had taken on full-time youth work without pay, travelling all over Kent. The amount of unpaid work done in Britain alone is colossal, from magistrates to those who reorganize and run abandoned railway lines. During my penurious days as a junior clerk, I helped to run a boys' club in the New Kent Road, a fairly rough district in South London. I tried to teach them boxing, which is partly the reason why I still find breathing through my nose a little difficult!

At home, too, I had to learn hard economic facts. The uncle who managed Dad's two shops in Walworth Road died, and Mother had to take over as manager. (The shops, incidentally, were a few yards from the famous inn assumed to have been referred to by Shakespeare in *Twelfth Night*. The words, 'In the south suburbs, at the Elephant', probably got the same sort of laugh as the comic in an English pantomime gets by quoting out of context a television commercial. Alternatively, it might actually have been the equivalent of a television commercial, a line slipped in, for a consideration, to boost the trade of the inn just down the road from the theatre in Southwark.) With Mother away most days keeping alive an unprofitable business, there was no high living at home. Food was good, but very plain. There was a lot of bread; and jam and marmalade were bought the cheap way, in stone jars holding seven pounds.

After we married in 1932, Constance and I only made ends meet by her careful shopping in Brixton Market, where 'fresh' eggs might be sixteen a shilling. (There was little refrigeration then, and you could buy 'new laid' eggs, or the staler and cheaper 'fresh' eggs.) Fresh herrings, cheese and vegetables were about the limit of our culinary aspirations, water or tea our vintage drinks, and bicycles our means of transport. We married on £178 a year; and when our son was born our income was only £210. We could not afford a daily paper. I walked part way to work to save a penny, and Constance soon afterwards made what seemed to her the ultimate sacrifice, the sale of her bicycle. Yet life had zest, and we have no regrets for those things.

I remember that in those early days someone said to us that the most fertile sources of human problems were sex and money. The friends we made through Moral Re-Armament were convinced that the heart of the money question was to be found in the principle of stewardship. If every bit of one's possessions was meant to be held and used as if one were a steward for God (or the common good, or however one cares to envisage it), it does help towards unselfish and sensible decisions. I must admit that it was simpler to apply the principle when our income was such that we had to count every penny than it is today, when we have a comfortable income. The principle, however, is the same. My wife and I still practise economies, do careful research before important expenditure, and consider often what we should do for others. For example, we make regular gifts to ten people who do, without salary, work which we regard as important, indeed essential, to society. I say this without pride, for we constantly wonder whether we should actually be doing more.

The real point of the matter is that if even most of us practised stewardship, on the basis of absolute unselfishness as far as we could see it, many of the things which harass us now would just disappear. Not long ago, the chairman of a very successful company became entitled under his contract of employment to a large bonus, based on the company's profits, and running into thousands of pounds. There was no doubt that he was entitled to it; but there were national wage restrictions in force for many workers at the time, and he was publicly attacked on moral grounds for accepting the increase at such a moment. In fact, the money had been paid some months before; and it was only after much publicity that, to reduce the temperature of those who were so vocal, the chairman let it be known that (whilst he felt it as right to accept the money as for any worker to accept a bonus) he had at once given all the money to charity.

I recall, too, a discussion on television about wage claims, when a Manchester docker said that he and (he thought) many others would be ready to forgo any increase if by so doing it would mean more for the worst-paid workers. 'What do you say to that?'

asked the chairman of Mr Hugh Scanlon, leader of the engineering union and another of the panel of speakers. Mr Scanlon said nothing—the one and only time I have seen him reduced to complete silence.

Nowadays, money does not only mean purchasing power. It also represents status, and recognition of a person's value in the eyes of others. One sees this in trade unionists' concern about differentials in pay for different types of work, as well as in the pay demands of top business figures. Yet all this can be overridden by a greater passion. If people are committed fully to some task, for ideological or other reasons, money takes second place, and may even be totally disregarded. It is not only men like Mahatma Gandhi and Vinoba Bhave who deliberately shun wealth and possessions. The hundreds who travel the globe for Moral Re-Armament, men and women, young and old, are all unpaid.

Gandhi, although he owned almost nothing in the world except a tin plate and an eight-shilling watch, regarded money issues as wholly subordinate to moral issues. He once wrote : 'The art of amassing riches becomes a degrading and despicable art, if it is not accompanied by the nobler art of how to spend wealth usefully.'

For myself, I have never had what the world regards as wealth, and am not likely to do so. For a few years, it is true, I have had a comfortable income—what Jane Austen called 'a competence'. However, the freedom I discovered in those early days, when we lived penny by penny, is still there, if I approach decisions in the same spirit as I did then. It began with an incident I remember very clearly, not long after I first heard of the principles of Moral Re-Armament, and started trying to apply them.

At that time, there were only a handful of people in our office, and there seemed to be no established method of regulating pay. It seemed to me that the way to get an increase was to go and ask for it. I suspected that some people did, and others did not, but I had no hard facts. I began to think that I was entitled to more than I was getting, and pressure began to build up in me.

If there were any rises in pay (and in those days of industrial depression it could not be assumed that there were), the people concerned were told of them individually on the last day of January. At breakfast on the thirty-first, I announced to my wife that if I didn't get a rise, I was jolly well going to ask for one. I even had the figure clearly in mind. She was strongly against my doing so. I suppose she felt that in the mood I was in, I was far from being absolutely unselfish. She would not let me leave for work until she had exacted a promise that at least I would not demand a rise without talking the situation over with someone who shared our beliefs.

Reluctantly, I left for work, and arranged to meet in the lunch-hour a man who was not much older than I, and worked in a small business near the Tower of London. I told him the situation, including how unreasonable I felt that everyone (including my wife) was being. He suggested we went back to his office for a time of listening. There, I sat with my mind in such a turmoil that I could get no clear thoughts at all. I told him so. He said : 'I just had two questions. Who does Frank work for? And who pays him?' As I looked at him, a torrent of thought went through my mind. I had made the decision, not so long before, that God should rule my whole life, so far as I could understand His guidance. That answered the first question. I also believed that God had created everything. The money was a token of part of His creation, and of His provision for His children. The situation suddenly looked quite different. I had to hurry back to the office, but I felt completely at peace. I felt sure that without aggressiveness on my part, Constance and I would somehow get whatever we needed to have. Anger and greed had dropped away.

Was the afternoon a fulfilment, or an anticlimax? I was called in and told I was being given an increase greater than I had intended to demand.

Some twenty years went by before I ever asked for more pay for myself, although I sometimes asked for more for others. This does not mean it is never right to ask. Later, I did, on two occasions at least.

In later years, I have often had to handle sums far in excess of my own resources, both in the firm and in connection with charitable trusts. It is usually right and necessary to use all one's business training, experience and shrewdness to use this money (as well as my own) in the best possible way—'the nobler art' of which Gandhi spoke. It is necessary, too, to have that freedom and certainty of basic principles which I glimpsed first in that office near the Tower.

I suppose the hatred some have for the profit motive is based on its association with exploitation. They are quite separate questions. In a bank in Bombay, I interviewed a senior official. He required help from his assistant, whom he bullied in a way which I found most embarrassing. 'You stupid fool' was one of the milder remarks. Four months later I was there again. The man who had been bullied was sitting in the number one man's chair. He addressed the man at his old desk with the same brutal scorn that had been served out to him earlier. During a wait, I asked him : 'Where is Mr Blank? Has he retired, perhaps?' 'No,' was the reply, 'he has not retired. He is on leave.' That is exploitation.

Elsewhere, I met two employers, who each had thousands of workers engaged in similar businesses. One of them paid good wages and gave all kinds of benefits to his workers in the way of schooling, housing, health services and so on, and gave liberally to charity. He was greatly loved. The other paid equally good wages, and was equally generous in all the same ways. He was cordially hated. Even one of his own managers told me so. Why the difference? I believe it was because the motives showed through. One did things because he believed them right; one simply did them because he thought he would gain from doing so.

It is natural to want to make profits, but Mahatma Gandhi's words cut near the bone. What are the profits to be used for when they are made?

To bring the subject back full circle, the profit motive is part of man's make-up. Like the sexual drive, it can be controlled, sublimated if necessary, or used in the proper way for creative purposes. It should never be ignored, and it cannot be destroyed. It is part of man's growth and development.

H

11

A Business Man's Politics

This chapter has caused me a good deal of difficulty. Writing it revealed in my make-up a thick stratum of cynicism and resentment towards politics and politicians. The only way to deal with this was to delete large parts of the first draft. I hope that, along with these passages, the unconstructive feelings also disappeared permanently.

Most of us sound off about politicians, and ignore the fact that the biggest thing wrong with politics is the lethargy of the ordinary citizen. Even politicians themselves do not pretend to perfection. They are supposed to represent the people, and perhaps their defects are largely reflections from those they represent.

For the record, I must say that in contacts with politicians I have always, I think, been met with courtesy, and usually with warmth and even enthusiasm for any suggestion intended to be helpful.

I am a Conservative, but perhaps not a very conventional one —if indeed there is such a thing. I have been in or drawn to the Conservative camp since as a schoolboy I addressed envelopes for election literature, when my father was a member of the Lambeth Borough Council. (My small brother showed a visitor a photograph of father in his fur-trimmed robe with the words, 'Look! it's edged with vermin.') On only one occasion did I vote Labour, in the 1945 election which displaced Churchill from the premiership. My motive was a half-baked idea that the others should be given a chance to show what they could do. And I later regretted it.

Although a member of the local Conservative Association, I don't stand for office in it. In general, I agree with the party's policies, or at least prefer them to those of other parties, but I do not consider that we are never wrong, or that we have a monopoly of truth.

Too much of the verbal enthusiasm for any particular party, and even for the democratic system itself, rings hollow in my ears. And far too much of the faith which people profess to put into political processes suggests to me a reluctance to take personal responsibility. Consider post-war Germany, after 1945. Everyone who gave the matter any thought wondered what would fill the huge vacuum left by defeat and by the discredit of National Socialism. Ernest Bevin, then Britain's Foreign Secretary, although a big man in every way, made speeches which at least implied that the mechanics of democracy were all that was needed to produce a new Germany dedicated to peace and social justice. Restore the ballot boxes, and all would be well. Yet effective power came near to being seized by the Communists through industry and the trade unions. At one point they provided over 70 per cent of the works council members in the major industries of the Ruhr. And this was when the political Communist Party was banned.

We need a broader participation in policy-making than a vote every few years. More people need to make their contribution towards sane and proper decisions by the law-makers.

I have, I must admit, done too little in this sphere myself, but I have written elsewhere* of how my business colleagues and I have tried to straighten out badly-thought-out drafts of laws in Britain and other countries. And we have been warmly thanked by legislators and civil servants for our attempts to help.

When I first moved into St Marylebone, our Member of Parliament was Sir Wavell Wakefield, the former England Rugby football international, later Lord Wakefield. During the blood-shed of the Cypriots' struggle for independence from Britain, press reports indicated that British policy was putting first the security of the British military bases. Adequate dealing with the demands by the Greek and Turkish Cypriots came second to this. I felt so strongly about it that I sent a lengthy telegram to Sir Wavell, saying that surely the first requirement of a military base was the support of a friendly population round it, so that the priorities would have to be reversed. As far as memory serves me,

* In *Ships That Go Bump in the Night.*

his letter in reply was as follows : 'I was most interested in your views on the Cyprus situation, and find myself very much in agreement with you. I brought your message to the attention of the Foreign Secretary at Twickenham last Saturday, during the half-time interval of the match between England and France, and I am sure he will keep these points before him.' This may be a particularly English way of dealing with foreign policy, but none the worse for that.

He was followed as member for St Marylebone by the Right Honourable Quintin Hogg, who had renounced his peerage in order to return to the House of Commons. He also was a very popular constituency member, and I remember with gratitude how he dealt with a personal appeal I had to make to him. A charitable trust of which I was chairman found itself in difficulty with the Inland Revenue, which raised an obscure and (in my opinion) stupidly wrong point of the law. As a result, the trust was unable to recover money due to it for about two years. A letter to our member of parliament (who was in opposition to the current government) produced a direct approach to the Chancellor of the Exchequer, and in a very short time the delays were ended and the money released.

It is hardly for me to attempt a portrait of this great and very human personality from my two or three fleeting touches with him. He tells his own story quite fully in his fascinating and challenging book *The Door Wherein I Went*. However, I may permit myself to tell of one other incident.

He complained that Marylebone is a difficult area for an M.P. to work in, as regards keeping contact with the ordinary constituents. It has a very quick turnover of its inhabitants, including students, and about a third of the population is said to change every year. On one occasion, when canvassing for votes in the day-time, he went through an entire block of flats and found only one living soul—a man trying to deliver a parcel. So my wife and I invited Mr Hogg to our flat one evening to meet as many of our friends and neighbours as we could cram in. He cheerfully agreed, and we managed to wedge over fifty people, by no means all Conservatives, into our drawing-room and hall.

He spoke briefly to each individual there, and then settled into an armchair, and talked, just as the spirit moved him, about a number of topics. It made such a deep impression on me that I think I can even risk telling some of it in an approximation to his own words, as I recall them.

In the previous government, he had been Minister for Education and Science, and he first talked of this, and mentioned his admiration of and confidence in most of the young people of that generation. Then he talked of the negotiations in Moscow for the first treaty to limit the testing of nuclear weapons. He had led the British delegation. This was long before any *détente* between the U.S.A. and Russia, and the two major nuclear powers were deeply hostile to each other. They were, in a sense, forced into a discussion by the intense public concern over the possible effects of radiation fall-out from indiscriminate testing of atomic bombs, but the prospect of any agreement seemed remote. Because we, too, had atomic weapons, the United Kingdom made a third party at the conference table. In Hogg's view, our presence had the effect of holding back both of the super-powers from completely intransigent stands on any point. And a treaty was signed.

Then he talked about France, and her great revival under de Gaulle, who had not long before said his famous '*Non, non, non*', to Prime Minister Macmillan's applications for Britain to join the European Economic Community. He said he had reasons to love France from his youth up. The new France under de Gaulle, he said, was out to reassert its standing in the community of nations, no matter if others were upset in the process. 'We find this very awkward and embarrassing at times,' he said, 'and it makes our ways hard. But when I think of the France of the nineteen thirties and the years just after the war, the corruption, the chaos, a new government every few months, then I glory in the advances France is making, however difficult it may make things for us.' It was something few Englishmen, and especially few politicians, would have said just then. It helped me to see how necessary it is for us to understand our nearest neighbours across the Channel. To bridge the gulf between the two countries is one of the deepest needs in Europe today.

Then he switched to a more personal note. 'I sometimes talk about the need for moral standards in society, in politics, and in personal life. Some people criticize this, they laugh at me, and say that I am pious. I don't mind that. I do try to be a Christian but, curiously enough, that is not the reason why I see the need for established moral standards. It is because I practised at the Bar for twenty-five years. There I saw a great deal of what turns people to crime, and in the Commercial Court I saw what makes for trouble and disputes in business and industry. I developed a deep conviction that if there are no standards of conduct which are generally accepted by all as being right, there is only one alternative way to regulate society. And that is force.'

What do I myself believe about politics? That is as hard to define as it is to state the policy of the Conservative party in one sentence, or indeed the policy of the Labour party. Quintin Hogg, Lord Hailsham, says in *The Door Wherein I Went* that in the days of the Tory Reform Committee of the nineteen forties he believed in publicly-organized social service and privately-owned industry. Now, both of the major parties seem to have developed into belief in (or acceptance of) a position where private charity fills the gaps in publicly organized social service, and where the state owns a number of major industries, and intervenes or interferes in others. Too often, it seems to me that policies have been based on expediency, even on sheer vote-seeking by both parties. Each seeks to draw support from every group in the nation, and amends its policies for this purpose. It has been said that the British have a genius for compromise, but it can also develop into a genius for confusion.

Most of us are aware of the deep divisions in policy in the Labour Party, some of them clearly traceable back to the conflict between the party's two early sources of strength and philosophy, first the nonconformist conscience of the early radicals, and later the Marxist doctrine of class war. We uneasily feel that there are equal divisions in Conservatism, though its earliest roots are not so clearly defined. The old characteristics of Toryism, the Established Church, the landed gentry and their tenants, and so on, persist in amended forms, but are qualified by many other streams of thought, reflecting the popular moods and demands of the last half century or more.

Socialism, to me, is an attractive ideal, but impracticable. One needs to remember that what we call the Communist countries call themselves Socialist. But even their own ideologists admit that they have failed in certain ways, particularly in developing people who really at heart put the community before themselves. They are also riven by ideological differences, of which that between the Russians and the Chinese is merely one of many. I feel that socialists of every kind underestimate two things, the amount of sheer selfishness in each of us, and the extent to which men can change for the better, given the right incentives. Because of blindness to these things, they rely far too much on changing the system, and delude themselves that if a good enough system is constructed, people will behave unselfishly. It is the old fallacy of trying to make people good by Act of Parliament.

I therefore prefer the more sceptical, pragmatical approach of the Conservatives. A vague but hopeful principle seems to me better than a rigid but misguided one. It may be, however, that we Conservatives are as wrong in our own way as Socialists are in another. Do we rely too much on freedom from restraint without giving care to develop the sense of responsibility which alone can keep freedom from being sheer licence, and even anarchy?

Although I find myself in the Conservative camp, there are two aspects of politics that I do wish my party and the others would quickly and decisively alter.

The first is that we have far too much government today. Statutes come out from Parliament in a torrent. Many of them are in skeleton form, stipulating that citizens must obey regulations which are to be drawn up later, and which are never properly debated. There is not a person in the kingdom who knows all the laws he is supposed to be obeying each day.

The millions who watched *The Pallisers* as a television serial will know that a hundred years ago Parliament adjourned in August, and might not reassemble till February. What a difference from today's crowded programmes of new laws, all-night sittings, and 'guillotine' procedure to limit debate! In Anthony Trollope's fiction, which was close to real life of those days, the Duke of Omnium's government fell partly because it had never passed a single piece of legislation to which it could point as an achievement.

I was relieved to read in 1975 that Mr Wilson's government had agreed to cut some bills from the plans for the next session, upon protests that not enough time could be given for proper consideration. This, however, is by no means enough. The leading article in

The Times of 20 November, 1975, on the Government's programme for the next session, said : 'The national interest would
be better served by Parliament ceasing to legislate at all for the
year than by Parliament enacting this cliquish rubbish. There are at
least seven Bills promised which are certain to do more harm
than good; some of them will do real and lasting damage.'
It may be flippant but it might, all the same, be sensible to suggest an all-embracing rule that no bill could be submitted for the
monarch's assent without a simultaneous request for repeal of two
existing Acts. There are plenty of useless old Acts available, and
it would make governments think a bit more before each new
one.

My second point is on a subject which is very topical—electoral
reform. The present system in the United Kingdom of a simple
majority in each constituency results in the differences between
the total votes given for parties being grossly exaggerated in the
numbers of members representing the parties to the House of
Commons. In the October 1974 election, the Labour Party gained
just over half the total seats on the votes of (I believe) 28 per
cent of the electorate, and 39 per cent of those voting.

Both the major parties are, broadly speaking, in favour of this
system, because each thinks it guarantees for that party a fifty per
cent chance of power. The Liberals and other minority groups
are furious and frustrated, because it reduces their influence in
Parliament to a token size. The Liberals propose a form of pro-
portional representation, where a number of constituencies are
grouped together, and voters are asked to put all the candidates
for all the seats in the order they prefer.

It is a little comic that the very politicians who oppose such
a scheme at Westminster insisted on the Irish applying a similar
scheme for elections to the Northern Ireland Assembly, to
strengthen the minority parties there. A member of that Assembly
told me that it was very difficult to work. In South Antrim I
believe eight constituencies were grouped together, and some
thirty candidates were supposed to be put in order of preference.

On the other hand, the present system at Westminster seems
to me most unsatisfactory. When one major party gives way to
the other, a large part of its time for the first year or two is spent
in reversing what was done by its predecessors. Moreover, a party

can only keep a majority in the House by appeasing all the different elements represented in the party, and this puts disproportionate power into the hands of extreme elements of left or right. They must be reasonably satisfied with the laws passed, or the Government falls.

A man in the aircraft industry told me that the disastrous state of that industry (except in times of war) was directly due to the fact that no government could plan for more than five years. It took ten years to mature a new aircraft, and no government would risk a decision because, if it failed, they had nothing to gain, and if it succeeded, someone else might get the credit. That was his opinion, anyway!

The argument for the present voting system is that an absolute majority is necessary for the Government to carry through its business. It might be much better if the Government carried through less business, and with much more compromise with the other parties.

However, the true reason may be slightly different. At an international conference recently, Mrs Indira Gandhi, Prime Minister of India, the largest democracy in the world, said something like this, 'Politics is about power. It is about getting power, and then holding on to it when you have got it.' Surely this is utterly wrong. Politics is or should be about how society ought to be organized. The personal status of politicians is subsidiary, and the good of the people should be the basis of everything.

In a democracy, close communication between the law-makers and those they represent has a profound importance. It is far more important than party—and on that subject Lord Hailsham quotes what Churchill said about the late Kingsley Wood: 'He was a good party man. By this I mean that he put his party above himself, and his country above his party.'

Having attacked the multiplicity of laws, I suggest a new one as a free idea for my own or any party. Instead of having a general election at periods of not more than five years apart, elect members for one fifth of the seats every year. (The roster of constituencies could be split into five in alphabetical order.) By this means the voters would have a much better chance of showing their opinions on how things were going in the country. There would be less risk, not more, of a small change in voters' views making for vast changes in policy. There would be a better prospect of stability in government, but if one opposition party began producing ideas to which the voters responded positively, that party could concentrate its work each year in certain known constituencies, and progressively capture seats until its strength in the House would make its plans effective.

We tend to over-rate the degree to which governments can effectively control events. Often, the groundswell of popular feeling and the action of individuals is much more powerful than the spray of debate or the splash of new legislation. A government finds it easier to hinder than to promote. For example, after the election in February 1974, heavier company taxation was brought in as a measure against inflation and its likely consequence of more unemployment. The result was that thousands of companies suddenly found themselves short of the cash they needed to carry on. Many had to apply to the Government for help. Some went bankrupt. There may be some extremists who rejoice every time a business fails and men lose their jobs, as another blow to capitalism, but one cannot think that these results were sought by the Wilson administration.

Many people think of the City of London as a political force. Quite wrong. The Lord Mayor and Common Council are limited to their local government of the 'square mile' and a few specific functions, such as health inspection of ships entering the Port of London. As a direct political force, the City can be pictorialized as a fraction of one member of Parliament. He represents the Cities of London and Westminster. Even the Governor of the Bank of England, who used to speak for the money market of London, is now a government appointee since the Bank was nationalized.

Can the financial interests in the City affect national issues? To a certain small extent they can, but only that. They are important more in supporting sound policies which work, than in resisting wrong policies. What happens in the City is much more the reflection of trends in the country, whether government initiated or not, than the cause of such trends. The money market and the Stock Exchange, whose index figures are so quickly headlined by press, radio and television, are like a barometer. They don't cause the weather in the country's economy, but they do register it.

Similarly, the foreign exchange market records what the world's impression is of affairs in Britain compared with other countries. When governments themselves find it practically impossible to control the movements in these markets, it is ludicrous to believe that private interests could do so. From time to time, of course, someone or other makes a big profit out of the situation of the day, whether it be foreign exchange rates, property values, or whatever it is. This can be damaging, in the same way as the London pigeons and starlings deface and even damage buildings. But it rarely goes on long enough or on a big enough scale to cause permanent effects.

One thing, however, is far more important than any of the points made above. People matter far more than systems. The things which count are the motives which control both the things we do and our omissions to do what we should. Ancient Athens invented democracy; but in the later history of the city state unscrupulous men manipulated the assembly to cause judicial murders, war, subversion and ruin. And the pride, lethargy and self-seeking of the majority of the electors let them do it.

In October 1974, when the Tories lost a general election for the second time that year, there was one development which I took as a sign of hope for the country as a whole. The leaders of both major parties predicted no improvement in living standards in the immediate future. Perhaps it was too much to expect more honesty, to admit that we could not really expect any improvement as far ahead as anyone could forecast, but at least it was to an extent more honest than for some twenty years. In that period, ever since Macmillan's disastrous, 'You never had it so good', every election had seen both Labour and Conservative manifestos saying to their supporters, 'Vote for us, and we will see that you get more without working harder.' We the electors greedily accepted this leadership, and looked for ever-increasing comfort and benefits. The more we got, the more we wanted. No wonder inflation ran riot.

It is true that living standards have risen in this country. There are more luxuries, and fewer poor. Perhaps no one now need be really poor, except by mischance. Many experts say these developments in Western countries have been made at the cost of a greater and greater gulf between their standards and those of the poorer countries. The worker in Asia or Africa who earns in a year what our factory workers earn in a week is staggered when the Englishmen go on strike for more. And a few individuals in Western countries have personal incomes which would be a large percentage of the budget of some countries in the United Nations. Miss Elizabeth Taylor, when remarrying Richard Burton, declined yet another diamond from him and gave its worth to pay for a new school in Botswana. Should one cheer, or weep?

The broader picture is that if mankind as a whole takes more and more from the earth in search of a constantly improving 'standard of living'—more and more things for everyone—we shall strip the earth of its resources, and make it uninhabitable. The Arabs and other oil-producing companies were the first to serve notice that exploitation of the poorer countries would have to end. They have done a service by raising before the eyes of all the limited amount of oil stocks, at a time when consumption was soaring.

It is becoming more and more important for statesmen, industrialists and the ordinary man and woman to give their attention to issues like these. The new perspectives this will give us may also make it much easier to deal with current difficulties in our industries, the balance of payments between countries, and all the other short-term crises which take up so much of our energy now.

What, however, will turn you and me and everyone else towards preoccupation with mankind's total needs, instead of our own? It is a very big change of attitude. Now and then one sees signs of it here and there. I personally have been fortunate to have seen it often where the ideas of Moral Re-Armament are actively at work, and being spread. I know there has been a basic change in my own outlook, what I have called a watershed in my living and thinking—however imperfect and incomplete the change may have been. I have seen changes in other people, sometimes dramatic and sometimes so gradual as only to be recognized by thoughtful contrasts between what was and what is. My friend Billy Arnold, a boilermaker at Harland and Wolff's ship-yard in Belfast, a lifelong Protestant, Unionist and Orangeman, says, 'I was brought up to hate the Catholics. Somehow, I don't feel that way at all now.' And he and his wife demonstrate this in all their daily affairs in that troubled city.

An entirely different type of man from Billy is Frits Philips, for many years head of the international Philips electrical organization, with factories in many countries. I have met him a number of times, once as far away as Japan. He ranges the world, and confers with premiers and heads of state, without ever losing his interest in the individual man or woman in the street. Among experiments in which he has participated are fascinating methods of having groups of workers take on together the making of, say, radio sets, instead of the repetitive work of the assembly line, and of putting the checks for perfect work on to the production workers themselves instead of using special inspectors. I do not know how successful these methods have proved in the long run, but I do know that his conviction is undimmed that, if industrial methods prove unsatisfactory, workers should not be forced to adapt to the methods, but the methods should be adapted to fit better with human nature.

In India once, I heard his son answering questions on his father's work and policies. One question was whether they had many strikes in their factories. The answer was that in the parent factory in Holland, there had only been one—and that was against the Nazi authorities during the Second World War. I read elsewhere that when the occupying forces took Frits Philips as a hostage for the good behaviour of the factory, six trade unionists went together to offer themselves as hostage if he could be released.

The year 1975 may be looked at by historians with respect, as the one which inaugurated a new world economic policy, the year when, first, the Commonwealth Prime Ministers meeting in Jamaica, then the Special Assembly of the United Nations in New York and the European Economic Community in Brussels, all agreed that the richer nations should guarantee minimum prices for raw materials, mostly produced by the poorer nations. It was a plan which united almost all elements in world leadership, and (temporarily at least) isolated and immobilized the few extreme elements who objected.

It was also a great contrast to the situation of only a year or two earlier, when a minority of 'developed' nations were steadfastly refusing the demands for united policies, and doing all they could to protect the basic advantages of their privileged position.

It can be argued that the change was enforced by growing pressures, of which confrontation with the oil states was the first major stage. For decades, oil-producing countries had demanded an effective share in deciding prices and the rate of extraction of oil, only to be denied. The great marketing interests, led by the huge multinational companies called 'the Seven Sisters', and representing in effect the consumers, made the decisions, including (since the prices included local taxation) the level of tax raised from oil by the producing countries. Little wonder that eventually the producing countries unilaterally seized control.

However, to attribute the new policy solely to such pressures, including action or the threat of action by producers of bauxite, sugar and other commodities, is less than fair to the many in all countries who genuinely wanted a fairer deal. It was widely recognized that economic aid was no substitute for the need for every country to pay its own way, even if this meant an end to the cheap raw materials for the highly industrialized countries.

To formulate a policy is one thing. To carry it out another. To make such a sweeping change effective called for a range of measures of great complexity and scope. Without them, the new policy would be rather like the small boy's definition of the equator. Mishearing his teacher's phrase, he said it was 'an imaginary circus running round the world'.

To remove the plan from the imaginary stage to the concrete, the first need was for a sweeping change in public opinion. What has been long accepted as right and necessary, must now be qualified.

For example, the whole doctrine of free enterprise and a free market has to be modified, or, maybe, re-defined in terms of a morality which has been to an extent ignored. English law (and so much in society is, in the final analysis, based on law) assumes that any contract is entered into by a willing buyer and a willing seller. The principle is based on assumed facts which nowadays rarely exist. One has only to think of tariffs, quotas, monopolies, economic blackmail, the multinational company which trades within its own network, the old colonialism's restraints and those of the new, with tied markets and ideological imperialism.

Similar forces operate domestically, with all kinds of official regulation, licensing, and outright prohibition of many kinds of deals. Compare the price of a piece of land where there is official permission to build on it, and the price without permission.

So, too, with ships. There is theoretically a free world market in ships, but it is confined by many local restraints. Laws or regulations regarding transfer of flag, or mortgages, make some deals impossible. The value of a ship in Moscow may differ sharply from its value in London or New York.

It is not too much to say that those countries which have benefited most from the concept of a free market have struggled hard to keep the idea alive, regardless of realities. Yet it is a great and even noble idea.

The two factors which have done most to foster the world's economic progress in the last two centuries are surely the Industrial Revolution and the free world market. Despite all their inconsistencies and failures, they have produced a better material life for hundreds of millions of people.

A good part of the nineteenth century was spent, in Europe and North America, in putting right some of the abuses of the Industrial Revolution, abuses in processes which began in the previous century. It took, I suppose, a century for the conviction to grow that it was wrong, and not right and natural, for small children to work in coal-mines, for women to toil sixteen hours a day in factories, and for workers to be bound body and soul to low wages, bad employer-owned housing, and employer-owned shops. The remedy was not to abolish the Industrial Revolution, but to outlaw the abuses. That was a long battle. Pioneer trade unionists and some humanitarian, far-seeing employers and politicians worked for decades before public opinion accepted that there were standards of right and wrong in these matters, apart from the blind working of economic forces. Only when the public conscience was aroused could laws be passed (and enforced) to give effect to the new ideas.

This latter part of our twentieth century may be seeing a similar process developing as regards the free world market. This is no longer fulfilling its purpose. In fact, the tendency has been for rich countries to get richer, and poor ones poorer. Trade between them, therefore, gets more difficult. It is a matter for argument whether the situation has deteriorated because of the intervention of governments, or in spite of this. It is not possible to stop the intervention of governments, so what now needs to be done?

Again, we must accept that laws or international agreements will not work unless there is the will to make them work—the conviction that the course of action is right. The decisions by the nations in 1975 were really the beginning of a general conviction that new principles must be applied to the market-place of the world. They accepted that the free action of economic forces alone could not be the means to meet mankind's economic needs.

What will be the means? I believe we must accept once and for all that it can no longer be taken as moral to buy always in the cheapest market and sell in the dearest. There must be a new measuring-rod, the consideration, 'Is it right?' Every bargain needs to be fair to both buyer and seller. It is as wrong to exploit a purchaser, as it is wrong to exploit an employee.

It would be folly to underestimate the size of the change needed, but it is a change which can be made. It is a question of applying the principle piecemeal in every situation.

In April 1976, I had a letter from an Englishman engaged in export trade with some of the rapidly developing countries. He is one of a team of three, English and Arab. On one basic issue he wrote (from Abu Dhabi):

'Surface superficial honesty is one thing, but absolute honesty is so uncomfortably penetrating, especially in business, that frankly I find it very difficult. Modern marketing is so competitive that the "little white lie" often creeps in, and I don't always have the courage to put it right.'

On the more general issue, he continued :

'Our decision to try and build permanent bridges between the Muslim and Christian worlds through business, on the basis of integrity and trust, is slowly beginning to work, both in orders and in human relationships. Most business men from the West come out here to sell what they have and make the largest profit. This has led to a considerable mistrust by many Arabs. What we need to do is to ask what do their country and people most want, and then to supply it at the right price, quality and delivery date.

'When I have expressed what our aims are, I have been moved by the response. Something of the heart happens, and trust is born. You feel that God is being allowed to work.'

An attitude like this could be the first sunshine in a new summer for world economic relationships.

Are these political issues? Not directly, perhaps, but they deeply affect the economics, the class attitudes, and the very stability of the modern state.

Change like that experienced by such men will transform the political scene, alter the sketchy and sometimes wrong principles we now apply, and give more hope for the future than political parties or policies which do not take into account such developments. In fact, such change could help to evolve parties and policies which are truly effective, and to make democracy really work.

12

Lawyers at Work

I count it good fortune that I have had so much to do with the law and lawyers. So many of us fear that world. I sometimes wish the lawyers paid more attention to overcoming that fear. The arcane language, the formalities and conventions, the time-wasting and above all the expense make a barrier between the law and the ordinary man or woman.

They also, on the other hand, have a curious attraction for people. A trial scene in the theatre, in a film, or on television almost guarantees success for the author.

Perhaps their very separateness, accentuated by wig and gown, helps to give people the wrong impression of lawyers. Sometimes, however, they are deliberately misrepresented.

At a dinner in the Queen's Room at the Baltic Exchange, I found myself near a man who was excellent company, full of fun and good stories. He makes sailing his hobby, I believe, like my brother, others of my friends, and half a million Englishmen. They are almost a breed of their own, and a very attractive one. 'They call me Black Jack,' he said at one point, with an appreciative chuckle. It was Mr Justice Donaldson, presiding judge of the Industrial Relations Court, the innovation of the Heath government which was quickly abolished by the Wilson administration which followed. Its total abolition was a deplorable result of doctrinaire politics, allied to a determination by certain trade union leaders that the privileged position of trades unions under the law should not be curtailed. The Industrial Relations Act had some undesirable features, which could have been removed, and which the Tories were ready to remove. It was a doctrinaire decision that the good provisions in the Act must go too, in a clean sweep, and later some of them had to be restored by the Labour Government.

At the time of that dinner, Sir John Donaldson and the court over which he presided were being abused by the extremists, as much as was the Act which he and the court had to apply. This clearly worried him not a bit. His duty was to administer the law as enacted by Parliament. The only regret he expressed was that the newspapers never mentioned the thousands of individual trade unionists who had benefited by the Industrial Relations Act. They had been given a remedy for such things as wrongful dismissal which they had never had before.

A section of the railwaymen had been causing chaos by a work-to-rule, including refusal to take out any train which had a minor, non-essential defect. Injunctions against this practice had been sought, and Sir John said that he had been sent by the cartoonist of the *Evening Standard* the original drawing of his cartoon about it. It showed a judge in full robes on a station platform alongside an engine, saying to the driver, 'I bet my rule book is bigger than your rule book.'

When the Act was repealed, and the Industrial Relations Court abolished, the Prime Minister remarked that it would free Mr Justice Donaldson for even more important work. I noticed that among the cases which fell to him to hear was the trial arising from the I.R.A. public-house bombings in Guildford and Woolwich. But I remember him more before he was elevated to the Bench, as a junior and then Queen's Counsel.

Two cases particularly spring to mind. One was a very abstruse question of marine insurance and general average, that old principle going back to Rhodian law, whereby sacrifices made for ship and cargo are paid for proportionately by both. It was a new point to me, and to the shipowner, the average adjuster, and the solicitor. We sent up the papers to John Donaldson in the Temple, and in due course we all met in his chambers. He was one of the few barristers expert in these unusual branches of the law. He said that he had considered the point, researched it thoroughly, and still had no idea at all what the law on it was. It was refreshingly honest. If we went to court, it would be to ask a judge to make fresh law, and to create a new precedent entirely. I think we decided it was not worth the expense.

The second case was very different. The facts were unique in my experience. A contract to charter a ship misdescribed the ship in a particular vital respect. We ploughed through a jungle of facts and arguments, and came to the conclusion that the shipowners' case had no merit. Then they came up with a surprising argument. They said both parties to the contract knew very well that the ship was not as described, and this had been done deliberately, to deceive a third party. They suggested that an application should be made to the court to rectify the contract, so that the ship was correctly described. This would put the shipowners in a better position. We were staggered, and said that we could not be associated with a move based on admitted dishonesty. Eventually, to dispose of the matter, we agreed that we would obtain for the shipowners the joint opinion of counsel. The opinion by John Donaldson, Q.C. and an experienced junior counsel was very short indeed. As I remember, it said : 'Clients are seeking an equitable remedy, which is only open to a party coming into court with clean hands. This is not the case here.'

Although in London the legal fraternity is large it is still a fraternity. I was once in court to hear an application to a judge for a certain order. In response to the affidavit supporting the application, we had lodged another affidavit made jointly by our solicitor, my late partner Cyril Miller and myself. Leading counsel against us was the Right Honourable Quintin Hogg, Q.C. Since his political party was in opposition and he was no longer in the Cabinet, he had returned to the Bar. As he rose, the judge said : 'Ah, Mr Hogg, I have before me here an affidavit made by Mr Cyril Miller. Before you open your argument, I should inform you that Mr Miller is personally known to me. It may be, therefore, that it would be preferable for your application to be heard by another judge.' 'Thank you, my Lord,' replied Mr Hogg, 'but I doubt if there is a judge on the Bench who does not know Mr Miller. I am very happy that your Lordship should proceed.' Cyril Miller had nearly twenty years of active practice at the Bar before he joined the family firm, so the comment was probably justified.

Mark Littman, Q.C., was another well-known counsel who appeared several times in cases for which I was responsible. One was the second 'Wagon Mound' case, in which the Judicial Committee of the Privy Council reviewed the whole principle of negligence and nuisance as actionable wrongs. He spent some days presenting the shipowners' case. On one day, I went to listen. As usual, the law lords interrupted counsel's argument whenever a point occurred to them, and he dealt with each with great courtesy and skill. Then one of them said something like : 'Have you considered whether the criminal law contains any useful parallels to the situation we have here ?' This was a real 'facer'. I had read the printed 'case' which set out both the facts of the matter, and the basis of the legal arguments. It was a civil action, and there was no word in it relating to criminal law. Mr Littman paused barely perceptibly, and said : 'That is a very interesting suggestion, my Lord. It raises very sweeping issues, and I do not feel I could venture to address your Lordships on it without first doing some considerable research.' 'Oh, never mind,' said the judge, and we got back to the main argument.

Another case in which he appeared on behalf of a shipowner insured by us was an important arbitration, held in the library of Gray's Inn. I will not identify the case, as it reflects badly on certain people, and even on the government of the country concerned—not, by the way, one of the 'flags of convenience' countries.

A smallish motorship had loaded a cargo of timber in Finland, late in the season, with short days and ice already forming in the anchorage. As customary, about a third of the cargo was loaded on deck. After she sailed, she ran into a gale and was at once in trouble. She took a list, some of the cargo went overboard, damaging the ship as it went, and sea-water entered the engine room. A radio message was sent out for help, and a salvage tug towed her into a Danish port.

The salvors demanded guarantees from ship and cargo to cover the sum they considered due to them, and these guarantees were given. The cargo interests, however, served a notice on the shipowners reserving the right to argue that the accident was the shipowners' fault and to hold them responsible.

Solicitors were instructed to make a full investigation into the facts. The salvage claim was disputed as to amount. It went to arbitration under Lloyd's Form of Salvage Agreement, and then one of the parties appealed against the arbitrators' award. All this took time.

Then the cargo owners issued a writ to recover from the shipowners for loss of cargo and for their share of the salvage award. They claimed that the ship was overloaded, and loaded in a way to make her unstable and unseaworthy. I sent for the solicitor, and asked to see the evidence he had got regarding the loading of the ship in Finland. He looked at me aghast. 'I haven't any,' he said. 'The statements I took start at the time when the gale blew up. I was thinking only of the salvage claim.' It was a scandalous piece of negligence by a man who was supposed to be a specialist in shipping law. But I should never have assumed that he had done what I had asked for. I should have checked it fully earlier.

I wrote myself to Finland, and got someone to enquire from the stevedoring firm which loaded the ship. It was run by a woman. Her statement was very short. 'We loaded the ship. I supervised it myself. The loading was perfect. All the ships I load are perfectly loaded and stowed.' When pressed for details, she remembered nothing. It had happened four years before.

The same was the case with the captain and crew. They remembered almost nothing about the loading. Our position was very weak. We made several attempts to compromise, but our opponents were belligerent in the extreme; and we finally decided to go on to arbitration, and to hope for the best.

The captain and chief officer were brought to London, and gave evidence through an interpreter. We were still moderately hopeful at the end of the day, although the captain seemed very hazy about such things as the ship's draft. Loading from barges in the near-Arctic night, with ice clinking against the ship's sides, did not help with accurate measurements.

The next morning, I had a panic call from the solicitor up in Gray's Inn. The captain had not appeared to continue his evidence. A telephone call to the shipowners' agents established that no one there knew where he was. Would I come up at once to discuss with counsel whether to make a last attempt to settle on any terms we could get? I took a taxi to Gray's Inn, and Mr Littman and the solicitor slipped out of the arbitration room to confer with me. Meanwhile, junior counsel dealt with a technical witness. Opposing counsel, Mr Henry Brandon, Q.C. (now a distinguished judge), had been very tactful about it all.

We decided that there was little to gain by attempting a settlement, and went on to the end. Late that afternoon, the captain turned up at the agents' office. He had thought his evidence had finished, and had gone shopping.

We lost, of course. The arbitrator's comments on the captain's evidence were scathing. He said that he did not seem to know or care whether his ship was seaworthy on completion of loading, or whether she was overloaded. He also, said the arbitrator, did not seem to understand the data on stability which he had on board. Mr Littman's rueful comment (counsel have to be good losers—there is a loser in every case) was that the only fortunate thing was that no one asked the captain what his job was at the time of the trial. He was in the safety department of his country's ministry of merchant marine.

I can only think of one other case in which a solicitor let me down over evidence. That was a different solicitor, and the results were even more unpleasant. It was a case involving three different parties. Our shipowner made common cause with a second party against the third. The second party collected the evidence; and, on the basis of what their solicitor told me about the evidence, I attempted a settlement of the case on a compromise basis. In the course of this I made certain statements about the facts which I afterwards found to be untrue. The solicitor had not in fact got all the evidence he had claimed to have. It was, I think, sheer carelessness, not deception; but it left me in a very awkward position. I went to see the man to whom I had made the statements, explained how it happened, and apologized; but I left with the nasty impression that he did not believe me.

Counsel may be good losers, but they rarely encourage litigation. Lord Justice Roskill, when he was still Mr Eustace Roskill, Q.C., told me that there had been a very big change in approach, even during his years at the Bar. When he started, he said, it had been 75 per cent litigation and 25 per cent advice; at the time he spoke, the proportions had been reversed.

Solicitors, too, shy off litigation. It is not (as you might think) a profitable aspect of the law for them. In litigation, they have to work long hours for a moderate fee. They are also very conscious that anyone involved in litigation loses something, if it is only a lot of time which he could usefully employ on something else.

I remember Noel Davies, a very senior City solicitor and a most charming man, doing all he could to persuade me not to fight a case about the technical unseaworthiness of a ship. A relatively small leak had done considerable damage to cargo. It was caused by the packing in a scupper-valve being put in slightly crooked during the annual freeboard survey on a British ship, the *Muncaster Castle*. A Clydeside shipyard did the work, in which all deck and shell openings are checked, and they slipped up on just one detail. Alas, I did not listen to Noel, and we had an expensive lesson. Even in such an extreme case, a shipowner may not transfer to someone else his responsibility to provide a seaworthy ship.

I remember, though, one claim which we were advised to resist, and in the end the other side did not sue. It was a claim against a ship for allegedly allowing excessive smoke to escape from her funnel, and so damage the stock-in-trade of a coffee-stall in the Rotherhithe Dock Road. It was investigated by a solicitor, the late R. A. H. Clyde, who enjoyed legal practice, and sometimes let his enjoyment show through. His formal opinion began by showing that it would be hard to show that smoke from the particular ship did the damage alleged. Then he went on : 'We will now consider the legal aspect. Assuming for the moment that the saveloys were more spotted than is their wont . . .'

Later in his career, when he was acting as arbitrator, I recognized his distinctive touch in a joint award concerning a Greek ship sunk by Israeli gunfire at Suez. One sentence read : 'Photographs of the ship after the attack are attached, *in memoriam*, to this award.'

Looking back, I can see a rich pageant of lawyers I worked with in many lands. A veteran Australian solicitor told me that he often briefed Bob Menzies before politics engulfed that versatile gentleman, who became a long-serving prime minister and ultimately Sir Robert Menzies, K.G. 'A brilliant advocate,' mused my solicitor friend, 'but a lazy lawyer.' When I made a brief visit to Istanbul, not long ago, a lawyer friend there apologized for not being free to be with me until the evening because, he said, 'I've seven cases in court today.' A lawyer we used occasionally in a certain European country was a regular *prima donna*. If things did not go as he wished, he staged a temperamental scene and had to be soothed down. His fees were enormous (but subject to negotiation). In fact, he once said to me : 'You know, Frank, I am a very *expensive* lawyer.' I replied : 'I know. We have been wondering if we can ever afford to use you again.'

In New York, with its maelstrom of maritime affairs, my firm uses members of several law firms. One of them, calling in St Mary Axe, said to me : 'I hope you are satisfied with the work we have been doing for you, Mr Ledwith.' I answered : 'Well, I am rather conservative. I am never satisfied about a lawyer until we have had at least ten years' experience of him.' His face fell. 'In that case,' he said in a subdued voice, 'I've still got about seven years to go.'

Three cameos to end with, two from the English courts, and one from a very different land. There can have been few men at the common law bar better known in his day than R. A. McCrindle, Q.C. (now working in Paris). Shortly after he 'took silk', we got involved in an unpleasant action which included allegations against my firm and against me personally. It was the kind of thing we could not let go, or compromise over. We had to fight it and win. For particular reasons, we used a firm of solicitors new to us then (although we have used them often since). They briefed Bob McCrindle, and in due course another partner and I went up to a conference with counsel in the Temple. Our solicitor preceded us into counsel's room, turned to introduce us as his clients, and was a little shaken when counsel spoke first, to say : 'Hullo, David. Hullo, Frank.' We had been in that room often, over all sorts of matters. The case was prepared meticulously, and fought hard. I, frankly, did not enjoy sitting in court and hearing allegations made against me; but as the days went on, it became very clear that the case against us was collapsing. Eventually, when all was virtually lost, leading counsel for our opponents made a speech to the judge which amounted to a plea for mercy, that we would make some small concession. McCrindle knew that, when our reputation was under attack, we could not do this. The judge asked : 'Well, Mr McCrindle, what do you say to this?'

Bob jumped up, with a swirl of his black gown, and made one of the shortest speeches on record : 'My Lord, my withers are unwrung.' We were given judgement on all points, a formal withdrawal of the allegations, and costs.

The second is an old story that my respected senior partner, Cyril Miller, was said to tell sometimes, late in the evening. When he was a very junior counsel he appeared before a strict and formidable judge, Mr. Justice Bailhache. As he rose to open his defence to the case, the judge looked down from the bench and said : 'Mr Miller, I see from the pleadings that you propose to argue six different alternative defences to this claim. I will hear you on any two of them.'

The third story comes from Iceland, where some two hundred thousand people, descendants of the Vikings, live hardy lives, fishing in the icy seas and farming in the glacial and volcanic valleys. Not many years ago, Constance and I had a memorable holiday there, spiced with a little business. We were lucky in that the ship which took us there, the little Icelandic liner *Sela*, was diverted from Reykjavik to two or three small eastern ports, and put us ashore at the 'northern capital' of Akureyri. There we were met by Valgard Briem, an old friend and my firm's lawyer, and his wife Benta, with a car. They took us back in leisurely fashion to Reykjavik, exploring a good deal of the north-west and west on the way. I find it difficult to restrain myself from rhapsodizing about Iceland, the mountains, lava-fields, glaciers, hot springs, salmon leaping in the rivers, rough-haired many-coloured ponies trotting on the stony tracks, and of course the people, self-reliant, hospitable, and often multilingual. But I am supposed to be telling a legal story.

One of many interesting things we did in Reykjavik was to see and hear a case in court. Valgard represented a shipowner. (He is one of the few Icelanders to have surnames; most have a patronymic only, Hallgrimsson or Fridriksdottir, and the telephone directory is indexed in order of Christian names.) The case concerned a seaman who had broken his arm on board, a common enough type of action in many countries. The whole affair was very ordinary, except that informality and brevity were obviously considered very desirable. The most unusual thing to me was the way that evidence was taken. Each witness was allowed to tell his own story, encouraged by questions if necessary. Both sides' lawyers were invited to ask questions then, to clarify points. Then the judge turned to the typist sitting alongside him, and dictated to her a short summary of the witness's evidence, which she typed direct onto her machine. She read it back to the two lawyers, who could challenge or criticize. But her script, amended, if necessary, was the record of that witness's evidence. It sounds cumbersome. In fact, it was very much quicker than the English system of mostly question and answer, with every word taken down at considerable expense. Somehow, it seemed to focus the minds of everyone on to getting a succinct and fair record of the evidence. At the end of the hearing, copies were ready for both sides, and for the court.

Another interesting thing about Iceland is that the very small population encourages those with special skills such as professional men to do several jobs. Valgard is a lawyer, average adjuster, and insurance-claims adviser to firms like mine; and, with another man who does the technical work, he runs a building association which promotes co-operative housing projects. Although a fairly young man still, he has in the past managed a fleet of trawlers, been buying agent for the City of Reykjavik buying everything from pencils to traffic-lights, and chaired the three-man commission which changed over all the road traffic from the left-hand to the right-hand side of the road. He also takes an active part in politics. Yet I find him as good a lawyer as many who give their whole working lives to the law. It must be the study they do in those long winter nights, just below the Arctic Circle.

13

Witnesses

In most lawsuits, there is another class of person sometimes more important than the lawyers—witnesses. They can be quite unpredictable.

Another of Cyril Miller's stories was of a collision case in which he appeared as junior counsel. The captain told the solicitors a story which in no way tallied with the known facts. They did their best to instil into him the basis on which evidence should be given, both in principle and in the circumstances of this case. In the witness-box, the captain went back into the fantasy world which he found more attractive and presumably felt would be more to his side's advantage. Eventually, the judge intervened :

'Before you leave the witness-box, Captain, would you mind telling me if I have correctly understood what you are saying? Your ship was proceeding northward in the Red Sea, and met the other vessel, travelling south. The ships were passing clear of each other at a distance of some two hundred yards. When they were level with each other, the other vessel suddenly moved sideways, and collided with yours. Is that correct?'

('A gleam came into the captain's eyes,' Cyril told me, 'and I knew that I was lost.')

'You may not believe it,' the captain said, 'but I saw it with my own eyes.'

We should not, perhaps, judge too hardly ships' witnesses who tell stories which are not believed. It is an unnerving business to be cross-questioned about navigation, stowage or seaworthiness, whether in private or publicly in a court room, and an officer or master may well feel that his job may be at stake. At one period it was the standing practice of some shipowners to discharge any captain who put his ship ashore or who was in a bad collision. No excuses were acceptable.

I handled a case once where a British ship was lost on the coast of Oregon. The currents and the direction of the tide vary a good deal in that locality, and the cause of the stranding was clearly a navigational error. However, as happens rather often in the U.S.A., insurers of the cargo brought an action against the ship-owners, claiming that the ship was inadequately equipped. Two points they made were that there was no spirit in the steering compass, and no wire on the sounding machine. (This was before gyro-compasses and echo-sounding machines were customary equipment.) Since the complaints were made following an inspection of the wreck months after the accident, I felt them to be rather stupid. Our lawyers told us that a local tribe of Indians had not unnaturally removed everything that was useful and portable. However, to defend the case, we had to call the captain as a witness. He had not been re-employed. We found him working as master of a tug in a small West Country port, full of resentment against his former employers, and quite unwilling to testify. However, we eventually convinced him that he should do so for the sake of us as insurers; and with his help our lawyers successfully defended the action.

Sometimes, on the other hand, the witnesses are over-zealous. A ship owned by a company I will not identify, except that I regret to say it is British, was in collision with another in the dredged channel leading to a certain port. The company's solicitor (who told me the story) examined the log-books and then interviewed the captain and chief officer. He explained that the story told could not stand examination in court. In the first place, the time taken from one point to another suggested that the ship was travelling at nearly double the maximum speed she had ever done in her life. Secondly, if a ship's helm is put hard-a-starboard in a dredged channel and kept like that for six minutes, she would finish up on dry land. The two officers explained that they had taken the log-books ashore, seen a local lawyer, and put in the story which he thought would be most helpful. After hearing the London lawyer's comments on such an attitude, they went away crestfallen.

First thing next morning they were again in his office, and proudly presented a new set of log-books, covering the entire voyage, and containing a new version of the collision. They had been up all night writing them out. Naturally, they had to be told that this was wasted labour. It was quite impossible to put these before the court, either. The claim by the other ship had to be settled.

This extraordinary piece of deception could be considered as an attempt to protect the men's employers, the shipowners. I have known, in nearly half a century's experience, a very few examples of deception being employed by crew members for a contrary purpose.

One was an action in New York for damage to cargo by fire. It is rare that a shipowner has to pay for this. Fire is such a desperate hazard that in many countries a shipowner is only held responsible for fire damage to cargo if it results from the shipowners' personal fault or privity. The ship was, to the best of my recollection, the motor vessel *Silversandal*, engaged in a round-the-world general cargo service. The ship's second engineer was called to give evidence on behalf of the cargo interests. He gave a lurid description of an engine-room almost swimming with oil, and with no proper upkeep, despite his protests to the shipowners. At the end of his evidence in chief, the shipowners' lawyer rose to cross-examine. At this date, I am unsure whether the lawyer was George de Forest Lord or his partner Allan Bradley, but it was one of these two. He asked: 'Is it a fact that on such and such a date, at such an hotel in Manchester, you told Mr H., from a firm of solicitors, that for the sum of £5,000 you would testify in favour of the shipowners?' The engineer looked round the court, saw Mr H. sitting at the back, and, after a long pause, said, 'Yes.' 'No further questions,' said counsel. The action, of course, failed.

The second case arose when a ship arrived in Venice, and was fined heavily for smuggling cigarettes. An officer who had been discharged went to the Customs and told them that, coming through the Mediterranean, the ship had stopped in the darkness off Sicily while a motor launch came alongside and took off a large quantity of cigarettes. We made a very detailed investigation, and decided that there was no truth in the story; but meanwhile the Customs had been paid (and kept) some £60,000.

A third was a ship with one of those proud names which seem unfortunate when something goes wrong. For example, the names of the great Niarchos fleet's ships include the prefix *World*. It was difficult to avoid a cynical trend of thought when, back in the nineteen fifties, the *World Concord* broke in half in a gale, and when the *World Peace* caused an international incident by knocking a railway bridge into the Suez Canal. The ship in this third case was not a Niarchos ship. She was owned by New York Greeks, flew the U.S. flag, and was named *Valiant Effort*. At the time, she was carrying a cargo of wheat to India under the American aid programme. She was chartered to the Indian government for the transport of the wheat, and such cargoes were not insured.

She met stormy weather in the Mediterranean. Off the coast of Tunisia, north of some islands, she hit a rock, possibly by 'bottoming' between giant waves. Water entered the shaft tunnel. The *Valiant Effort* was one of the standard war-built ships, with engines amidships, and it should have been easy enough to close off that steel tube in which is the shaft connecting the engines with the propeller, simply by closing the watertight door. However, water entered the engine-room, and got deeper and deeper; the boiler fires were extinguished, all power was lost, and the crew took to the boats in the darkness.

They were lucky. A French aircraft carrier heard the S.O.S., and at daybreak helicopters picked up the entire crew from the sea. The ship surprisingly did not sink, but drifted in a waterlogged condition on to the sandy Tunisian coast. After an unseemly altercation between a possible salvor and the local authorities, no salvage attempt was made. There she remained, to be slowly engulfed in the sands.

As a precaution, we flew out a London solicitor to investigate and record the facts before the crew were repatriated to the United States. It appeared that the watertight door had jammed open, and that this turned an accident into a disaster.

Some months later, lawyers acting for the Indian government started an action before the New York courts against the shipowners, claiming a million dollars for the loss of the cargo of wheat. We learnt with concern that members of the crew had stated that the bulkhead between engine-room and shaft tunnel, which should have been watertight, had open holes in it, through which passed various cables and pipes. These holes were of course supposed to have been a watertight fit round the cables and pipes.

The story seemed very unlikely to me, for the ship had been inspected for seaworthiness by the United States Coast Guard just before the voyage. Such inspections are very strict, and the officials confirmed that they found the bulkhead and door in order. We instructed David Wood, a vigorous young lawyer, experienced in litigation, to defend the action, and arranged with him that we should send a London naval architect and marine engineer, Carlton Garratt, to examine the wreck.

When he returned, his report was disappointing. The wreck could conveniently be reached only by launch. Garratt had got on board, but found the engine-room half full of sand and water, so that he could see nothing. We had to send him out again with a diver. I think the diver's name was Mears, but I remember better his blue eyes, weather-beaten face, and quiet voice, a great contrast to Garratt's animated face and quick, high-pitched speech. Mears had been a senior Royal Navy diver, then worked with Siebe, Gorman & Co., who make diving suits, smoke helmets and such gear, and finally became a consultant on underwater matters.

Back in Tunisia, they hired a large launch and a pump and tried, without success, to pump out the engine-room. However, they did manage to shift enough sand to enable Mears to go down and reach the watertight bulkhead and door. He could see nothing, with the pump working to keep sand and water circulating, but he produced an exact report and sketches of what he found. As he told me later, 'We divers are quite used to seeing with our hands.'

The steel door was oval in shape, and secured when shut by six clamps. Most of these were securely in place, but one was jammed on the engine-room side of the door, and the door itself was twisted. Obviously force had been used to try to clamp the door tight; the inrush of water and perhaps a touch of panic had concealed the fact that one clamp not only could not be closed, but was actually obstructing and distorting the door itself. Mears also traced with his hands the various pipes and cables passing through the bulkhead, and confirmed that they were held in place by tight collars, with no gaps round them.

His information was passed on to the opposing lawyers, but they insisted on pressing on to a hearing. We therefore had to

fly Mears out to give verbal evidence in support of what he had
written and drawn. The judge believed him, rejected the other
evidence, and gave judgement in the shipowners' favour; for
under the laws of most countries a shipowner is not liable for a
cargo loss resulting from a simple error in navigation or management of the ship by one of the crew.

Why did the crew members give false evidence? It might have
been malice. More likely, they did not know it was false. The
men struggling to shut the door were in a jet of cold sea-water,
a strong jet, for this would be twenty feet or more below sea-
level. They were in danger of drowning and possibly of a boiler
explosion.

They say that if six people see a road accident happen, they
usually tell six entirely different stories of how and why it happened. The men in that engine-room would be in a far less suitable position to give an accurate and coherent account.

This is the first thing to realize when you are dealing with witnesses. I once sat by while a statement was taken (by an expert in
the craft) from a Portuguese captain who had been in a collision.
In the first hour, the only clear facts which emerged were that his
ship's whistle signals woke him up, and he rushed up on to the
bridge in his pyjamas, with bare feet. And it was cold. It took
several hours more of patient work to clarify what he heard and
saw.

Once I spent nearly a week with a surveyor, recalling from the
depths of his memory every detail of what happened when a certain ship was inspected several years before.

On the other hand, I might quote a story told me by A. C.
Hibbard, who in his long career with a City firm of solicitors has
probably taken more statements than I have eaten hot dinners.
His very first attempt, as a lad of seventeen or so, was to get a
statement from the second officer of a ship then in the London
docks. He found the ship, got on board, and found the man. 'I'm
just going on leave,' said the officer, 'I can't waste time on this.'
Hibbard offered to talk as they went, and the pair set off. Outside
the first public house, the officer said : 'Come in and have a drink.'
Hibbard, a carefully brought-up young man, had never been in
a pub in his life. He hesitated, and then said : 'Perhaps I'd better
wait for you outside.' He stood on that cold corner for three solid

K

hours. Then the officer came out. 'What? Are you still here?' he asked. 'Well, if you won't drink with me, I won't talk to you.' And he walked off.

This story is not inserted to boost the pub trade, but to show that witnesses are human, with ordinary human failings, just like yours and mine. They may take offence, get scared, become confused, and in all honesty make mistakes. Much of the time, the truth comes out in spite of all these things.

Three things I have learnt to watch for in witnesses with whom I have had to work. One is fear. It may well be fear of losing one's job, or (in the case of a captain or officer) his 'ticket', the certificate of competence which may be withdrawn or suspended for a period.

Another is vanity. I remember one expert witness who threw away the main part of our case by suddenly giving in the witness-box an opinion the opposite of the one he had given us earlier, both verbally and in writing. I put it down to vanity. He thought we were losing the case (we were not, until then) and he did not want to be heard advocating a course which would be found by the arbitrator to be wrong. Later, he submitted a bill for his services exceeding the fees of the Queen's Counsel who prepared and argued our entire case. When I pointed this out, he had the effrontery to say that his own services were more important than those of the Q.C. I paid him, as far as I remember, half what he demanded, and never employed him again.

The other thing is of course crookedness, but that is another story.

14

There Was a Crooked Man

There was a crooked man,
Who walked a crooked mile,
And found a crooked sixpence
Upon a crooked stile.

So runs the nursery rhyme. I have met that man, or one like him,
a number of times. Anyone who meets a wide range of people is
sure to do so.

I am not thinking of a person who merely makes a slip. Most
of us do this. A man I knew and respected in the City for many
years, and whose memory I still respect, did so twice. On one
occasion, he made an intemperate remark about a certain race of
people (in a flash of irritation, I believe) which resulted in a
humiliating rebuke from a judge when the matter was taken to
court. Later, he was careless with his accounts. Neither of these
things should have happened, but he was no crook.

A story which was told often years ago about a certain solicitor
would indicate that he was a crook—except that I do not think
the story was true. It was told, I believe, for fun, and for effect,
and perhaps with some malice, by rivals he had worsted in the
courts. I never met anyone who believed it, though some thought
there was a tinge of truth in it, just enough to make the wild story
really funny. The man in the story, whom I remember (he wore
a beard) but will not identify, was a specialist in lawsuits arising
out of collisions and salvage of ships. Whenever the accident
occurred in the winding, crowded reaches of the River Thames,
the lawyer (it was said) had an uncanny knack of invariably finding an independent witness, someone not employed by or financially connected with the shipowner involved. This independent

witness was a rough, tarry waterside character, who just happened to be on the end of the jetty (perhaps in the middle of the night) watching the shipping. He saw it all happen, and his description was always extremely helpful to the party our friend was representing.

It was even alleged that there was a whole group of these characters, who appeared before the court in strict rotation, as different cases came up for trial. A variant of the tale added that on one occasion the solicitor was heard addressing an independent witness in the corridor of the court, before he went inside to give his testimony : 'Now, look here. I've got your evidence here, all written down. Our counsel, the chap in the wig on the left side of the court, has got a copy, too. And I warn you, if you say one single word that's not written down here on this proof of evidence, that's perjury.'

A man whose actions spoke clearly for themselves was the central figure in another case. I never met him, and dealt with him only by mail and telegraph, through a firm of Lloyd's insurance brokers who had introduced the business to us a year or so earlier. The man was a citizen of a certain South American country. His father had actually been president, and (some said) the most successful president in history. It depends what standards are used. He was said to have left the country before the inevitable revolution, with some eight million dollars.

The ex-president's son controlled a shipowning company, and an insurance company, both of which were concerned in the tankship which figures in this story. The shipowning company insured the ship's hull and machinery for all marine risks with the local insurance company, which in turn reinsured the ship with the London market, but *only for the risk of total loss of the ship,* at a fraction of the original premium. The shipowners' liabilities were insured with us.

The curtain went up on this drama with a report through the brokers that the ship had been aground in the river at a not very accessible South American port, and had also had a fire in the crew's quarters. Further reports said that the damage was severe, and then that it was so extensive that the ship was considered a total loss. The shipowners cabled that they were proposing to pay the crew the two months' wages due to them upon the wreck of the ship. I replied that I was sending a representative to the spot so that we could have a direct report, and asked for full documents by airmail. It was at this point that I began to sniff the air. I enquired, and was told, about the insurances on the ship herself.

The man I instructed to fly south from the Panama Canal Zone reported that the ship was now anchored in the river, and his non-technical eye did not consider she was a total loss. He asked for a marine surveyor to be sent. Enquiries in London showed that there was a suitable man in Jamaica, not too far away. So I went to see the marine claims adjuster of the company which led the risk on the reinsurance on the hull and machinery. (The leading underwriter, the first man to accept part of the risk on a marine insurance cover, takes the initiative on claims, and the rest usually follow his lead.)

I suggested that we should share the cost of sending a surveyor to report as to whether the ship was a total loss. All the information supplied from the insurance company in South America said that this was so—but this company was closely identified with the shipowners. The London man was worried, but he considered himself bound by the conventions of the London insurance market. It would not be proper, he thought, for him to send a surveyor. A reinsuring underwriter relied on the primary insurers for information.

This convention did not apply to my firm, which was itself the primary underwriter for the liabilities, so I spent some hundreds of pounds on getting a surveyor there. Meanwhile, a claim had been made on us for crew expenses (some had been injured, it was said, and all had to be maintained in the port at some expense), for the two months' wages (though no receipts were attached), for a considerable sum of ship's cash said to have been destroyed in the master's cabin, and other items. What had seemed earlier to have a suspicious smell now stank horribly.

The report eventually came to hand from the surveyor. The ship, old and dilapidated, had suffered some damage. The bottom had not been seen, but leakage was only slight. In his opinion, there was no evidence to suggest a total loss. If dry-docking showed bad bottom damage, it might possibly be different; but there was no dry-dock in the port, and the shipowners refused to move the ship.

I offered to pay some small items of the owners' claim which seemed proper, and others which were a little doubtful, but declined to consider the 'lost cash', or the two months' wages, and some other charges. There was a handsome row. I sent the papers to an independent average adjuster, who agreed with me. The owners threatened to sue. I agreed to an arbitration, and the arbitrator also agreed with me, so the shipowners only got those expenses I had admitted originally.

Meanwhile, the insurance company in South America announced that it had paid a total loss, and called upon the London reinsurers to pay 'as original', in accordance with their contract. In my opinion, the London men had tied their own hands. They were not, apparently, prepared to fight the claim, for this would be an outright charge of fraud. In the end, they compromised, and paid 70 per cent of what was due for a total loss. In justice to them, it should be said that marine insurers in London have often paid part or whole of a doubtful claim, and are sometimes generous in border-line cases.

However, a report relayed to me from South America said that, as soon as the 70 per cent was paid over, the ship got steam on her engines, raised her anchor, and left the port.

Some forty years ago, when G. H. Vos was the partner in the Miller firm responsible for appointing the firm's representatives abroad (and for ending their appointments if necessary), he told me with some consternation that one of these correspondents had been making money 'on the side' in cases he had handled for us. He charged us a fee; but, in respect of repairs to a wharf damaged by a ship, he had also collected a commission from the repairers. Mr K., said Vos, was to visit the office in the near future and, said he, 'I'm going to charge him with this, fair and square.' He duly did, and told me afterwards, in a blend of indignation and amusement, what had happened. Mr K. had shrugged, spread out his hands, and said : 'What can I say? It is true, of course. But as long as I represent you in my city, only one person will swindle you.' We kept him on. The fact was, said Vos, we did not know anyone else in that port who would even give us that limited undertaking.

How does one spot a crook? I am not sure I am a very good person to pontificate on that. I have been surprised more than once. A man I had known for nearly twenty years and never suspected of anything odd, suddenly moved out, leaving his firm short of over a million pounds. Another man I know was widely, even generally, alleged to have milked his company of its assets, and to have stowed the money away in numbered, untraceable accounts in Switzerland. In fact, he did nothing of the sort. I had to work, for certain reasons, with a professional accountant to examine his affairs minutely—it took a number of years—and there was not the slightest trace of defalcation. There were mistakes, but no dishonesty.

Some danger signals are very obvious. If someone you do not know sits down opposite you, and says at an early stage of the conversation, 'I'm an honest man,' you should keep a firm hand on your wallet. If he had been an honest man, he would never have said so.

Eyes and hands often signal things opposite to what the words are saying. So do tones of voice. The crook is sometimes shifty-eyed. Sometimes he looks at you with a straightness and openness which is a little unnatural.

He will also press his points, at times, harder than is necessary. A man tried very hard once to get me to pay £4,000 for expenses incurred in sending home various seamen discharged in different parts of the world. If they were discharged through sickness or injury, then we should pay, but there was nothing to show that the men were not repatriated simply because their period of engagement had expired. He pressed me; and when I would not yield, he went off, and returned with two others, who joined in haranguing me. They threatened to complain to my boss, and to take away all their business. I was youngish then, and what my boss would say, I did not know. I felt scared, but said : 'As far as I am concerned, I don't want to have your business, except on an honest basis.' In the end, they gave up, and got fuller details from abroad. My suspicions had been right. The claim was scaled down to £1,200.

The curious sequel was that we were better friends afterwards than before. They respected my attitude, and they knew very well that I watched carefully everything they did.

'It's a question of principle', is another phrase I listen for. Crooks use it : but so do others when they want their own way. I remarked on one occasion, 'The only principle I can see in this situation is that Mr Blank' (the man who had used the phrase) 'is always right.' It can be self-will. It can be vanity. I can tell you that from my own personal experience.

Another characteristic of the crook is the reluctance to put things plainly in writing. He prefers to deal by word of mouth, without any third person present. If he writes at all, it is guarded, or vague, or with its meaning lost in verbiage.

Reputation, again, is a surprisingly useful test. 'Love is blind. but the neighbours ain't.' A big group of ships, controlled by an able, strong-willed man, transferred their business to us. On renewal of the insurance for the second year, we took into account, in fixing the premium, the owners' estimates for claims pending, on which we did not have full data. The claims turned out to be much higher. Next year, we added a margin to the owners' estimates. It was not large enough. The third year they tried it again, and we said that we could not accept their estimates. We soon lost their business. Now every important insurer in London avoids insuring this group. Some have had experience of their methods. The others wonder why so many of their colleagues don't want the business.

I have left until last what I feel is the clearest evidence possible of a crook. What effect does he have on you? When you deal with him, do you feel yourself tempted to compromise on what you feel is really right? Do you begin to cut corners, and to think that it does not matter very much if you give a little more than you should? If so, there is a crook about. Be careful there are not two.

Then, if you have detected a crook, how do you tackle the situation? I am not thinking of crime, a matter for the police, but business dealing which is within the law, yet crooked. The only way, in my view, is to study the man, and base your action on that study. The action may be different each time. But certainly a crooked man should not get away unshaken and unscarred, if you can help it.

One man who pressed a dishonest claim we tried to convince by argument, or to find some way of accommodation, but he was so elusive and supple in his moves against us that we decided on outright confrontation. The lawyers were called in. Every time he moved, we hit back twice as hard. It was costly in time and effort, but in the end he gave up completely.

Another very subtle and powerful opponent was dealt with in quite another manner. Patience was our main weapon. One day I listened to him for four hours, saying almost nothing myself. Sometimes months went by without any development. I took no initiative at all myself, but when opportunity served, I sealed off part of his manœuvring area by getting a written agreement, or a verbal one before witnesses. Eventually, he found himself penned in a corner. Several times he tried to break out, but could not. In chess, a stalemate is a draw, but in business it can be a win. It leaves you free to get on with something more productive.

A third type of man, I would ignore. I once wrote : 'We understand your game, and we do not propose to play it.' Subsequent letters from him on the subject were not answered. Our position was strong, and he could not breach it, however cunningly he probed, if we kept our defence intact.

Where it is possible, one should try to win a difficult man, whether crooked or not, to a better way of acting. Character may decide how a man acts, but if he is constrained into right action over a period, this actually affects his character, in many cases. It is rarely right to shun a man because you do not like his morals and methods. He may not be the kind of intimate you would select, but exclusion is no answer. (Similarly, I once suggested to my Member of Parliament that our country's foreign policy should regard every other country either as a proved friend or as a potential friend.) Often, I have known a man of doubtful morals do something generous, unselfish or honest for the sake of friendship. Such an act is sheer gain.

A friend, according to one definition, is someone who knows all your faults and still likes you. In dealing with crooks, it is wise to be prepared (and if necessary protected) against any trick they may try; but the real question is, 'Who changes whom?' Do they lead you, insensibly perhaps, into lowering your standards, or are you honest enough to convince them that it is better to be so?

15

Oil and Other Pollution

So much hysterical and ill-informed nonsense has been written about oil pollution that one is reluctant to dive into the subject. The only justification is perhaps an endeavour to restore a sense of proportion.

To start with, my own opinions are first, that oil pollution, though serious, is not nearly so grave a problem as some make out, and second, that some other forms of pollution are far more dangerous than oil, and more dangerous than most people imagine.

My involvement in the subject goes back a good many years. In the nineteen forties and fifties we were paying frequent claims for damage to property by oil discharged into rivers or into the sea. For example, a tanker owned by Compañía Shell de Venezuela was loading crude oil supplied by the same company at a berth in Lake Maracaibo. There was a misunderstanding between ship and shore, and as a result 1,200 tons of oil were discharged into the lake. We paid literally hundreds of claims for cleaning up fishing boats and nets. At one point, our representatives on the spot said that it looked as if we would have a claim from every fisherman within a hundred miles.

Then, as increasing penalties were imposed in different countries for the escape of oil, we paid more claims for these fines. Many people (including other insurance men) find it strange that the mutual P. and I. clubs pay shipowners' fines for them. The basis is that a shipowner sitting in Paris, Oslo, or Karachi cannot ensure that his captains, and crews thousands of miles away do not infringe the laws where they happen to be. The penalties, on the other hand, are imposed on the shipowners, not on the guilty or negligent men, because it is easier to collect a large fine off the shipowner, whose ship is subject to arrest, than from a possibly spend-thrift seaman. The clubs are particular what they pay. They do not cover fines for the personal faults of the shipowners, and in no case do they pay fines for overloading ships.

A third way in which we are involved financially is in 'clean-up' expenses. This is partly in an endeavour to minimize fines and claims for damage to property, and partly because in some countries shipowners are compelled by law to clean up after oil spills.

Mention oil pollution to the average person, and you get one reaction every time—*Torrey Canyon*. My firm was fortunately not concerned with the wreck of that tanker, the oil drifting on to the English and French coasts, and the subsequent claims, enforced by the arrest of sister ships in Singapore and Rotterdam. Several millions had to be paid out.

In the copious television coverage at the time, as the Royal Air Force bombed and set on fire the stranded vessel near the Scilly Isles, it was difficult to avoid the cynical thought that the British Government's calls for immediate action on the incident itself, and for introduction of penal laws in the future, were louder and more strident because the wreck was so near to the Prime Minister's holiday home.

Not many months later, another major incident occurred on the coast of Puerto Rico, at the very time that President Lyndon B. Johnson was visiting there. With a major oil spill right under his eyes, he also spoke loud and long. An election was due in the near future, too.

Suddenly, everyone was calling for action, both legal and technical. Some of the first hurried steps were most unfortunate. It may well have been quite wrong to bomb the *Torrey Canyon*. Certainly, other measures taken to dispose of that ship's oil slicks were a mistake. The liberal use of detergents is now said by scientists to have done far more damage to marine life than the oil could ever have done.

A BP man told me, too, that the way the detergents were employed was wrong. The launch owners were paid so much a trip. They just emptied the drums over the side, and hurried back, when the stuff should have been dribbled into the oil slicks, with the launch propeller at slow speed beating the oil and detergent together into a relatively harmless emulsion. Naturally, better techniques have been developed since and the present-day dispersants are said to be 1,000 times less toxic.

This does not mean that immediate action is necessarily wrong. When two Chevron Oil Company tankers collided under the Golden Gate Bridge in California, the company itself took immediate action to deal with coastal pollution, and so did all kinds of volunteers. Their help was welcomed by Chevron, who paid all reasonable expenses. They also gave leave (as one of their engineers told me) to any of their own staff who wanted to lend a hand. I saw some of the accounts which were settled by the company, and was touched by the meagre sums involved, though the total was very large. One girl claimed for replacement of a T-shirt and a pair of jeans, apparently her complete oil-fighting uniform. Another asked for ten dollars for a doctor's fee. Her face had been pecked by an oil-soaked sea-bird.

The beaches must have been quite a sight, with everyone helping, from experts with modern equipment to barefoot students and hippies.

It may not be generally known that nearly all owners of tankers have joined in a voluntary scheme to pay for the cleaning of oil spills, over and above their legal liabilities, and the oil companies as owners of the cargoes carried also have a scheme. Many millions of dollars have been spent voluntarily in this way.

The loss of the *Torrey Canyon* and other accidents following that one produced an almost hysterical rush to bring in new penal legislation. Fortunately, some of the earliest and most extreme ideas were modified. Mr Wilson and his United Kingdom Government referred the matter to the United Nations, and without too much delay the appropriate body produced an international convention on legal liability for oil pollution which was adopted by many countries, and proved workable.

In the United States, some politicians at first called for unlimited liability of shipowners for damage done and clearance costs, whether or not there was any fault by the shipowners or their employees, and for proof of insurance against these liabilities as a condition for allowing any ship carrying oil as cargo or fuel to enter American waters. Fortunately again, the responsible committees of the Senate and House of Representatives heard evidence from London insurers (including my firm), and realized that it was not possible to get insurance for an unlimited sum against what would be (in case of a spill) a certain liability. Some limits were therefore set.

Later, one or two States tried to show their zeal by passing laws more strenuous than the U.S. federal law; in one case, the governor of the State was sued on a plea that his new law was unconstitutional. Some other countries, too, have introduced laws acutely penal in nature—and some had second thoughts about them later. At the time I write, a few countries have laws which are too extreme; many have laws which are workable; some have none on this subject.

Too extreme? If a country puts too costly liabilities on ships which visit its ports, the cost of insuring against these liabilities may be so high as to affect that country's trade adversely, and put an unreasonable burden on to the cost of living there.

Oil pollution has been with us a long time. On a family holiday at Looe in Cornwall in 1946, we found the beaches liberally smeared with black oil residues, traceable to the sinking of ships in the 1939-45 war. Old maritime characters told us that they could remember similar, if lesser, trouble at the end of the 1914-18 war.

When I visited Tokyo in 1962, lawyers there were acting for us on claims arising out of a tanker going aground in Tokyo Bay. I was inclined to treat it as greatly exaggerated, but the lawyers told me that the claims must be taken seriously. In the bay, fishermen had developed quite extensive cultivation of shell-fish and edible seaweed, and much damage had been done to these beds. Moreover, the members of the fishermen's co-operative, some 1,800 strong, had threatened, if their claims were not met, to occupy the lawyer's offices, and sit there until satisfied. And they meant it. We had to pay out a large sum.

About the same time, I dealt with a claim from Italy for damage by spilt oil to mussels which were grown in that area on rows of sticks planted in shallow parts of the sea. I believe they use a similar method in Australia for oysters.

The recent relatively sudden roar of complaint and prodigality of action in this connection is due in part to the far greater quantity of oil carried by sea, in part to the huge amount often carried in a single ship today, and in part to the growing concern about the human environment.

The climate of opinion sometimes produces bizarre and even comic claims. For example, a ship was in collision in a river in northern Europe, and oil escaped. A federation of duck-shooting clubs complained that oil in the marshes had ruined their sport, and claimed heavy damages. A colleague of mine went out there, met a bunch of angry sportsmen, and started asking them questions. He asked how many duck had been shot in the last three years, how much they were worth at market prices, and how many cartridges were expended, and at what cost. It was the last two of those questions which caused the furore. The number of cartridges expended, on an average, to dispose of one bird was so large as to give a very bad impression of the standard of marksmanship. Rather than discuss these matters in court, the claimants accepted a very reasonable settlement.

It must be admitted that oil pollution is a serious problem. It has killed thousands of sea birds and destroyed other marine life, fouled ports and pleasure resorts, and occasionally produced a fire hazard. Just how serious it is, is difficult to establish. Some scientists think no warnings can be too doom-laden. Others think that the sea can absorb most of the oil, given time. In time, even the beaches clean themselves. But I can think of one writer who suggested that constant small spills in the Agulhas Current, off South Africa, could be causing an accumulation of oil in the Antarctic. This might, he suggested, reduce the vast flow of plankton from that region which is a very vital part of the cycle of life through the different levels of the oceans of the world.

So it might, but there is no proof that it is so. One could also argue that if the pollution goes on, and the damage is done, it will then be too late to reverse it. But nobody knows. This is only one aspect of the sea's mysteries, which we deeply need to explore.

To my mind, there are many more risky things than oil travelling across the sea, or even being dumped into it. Radioactive waste from power stations falls into this class. So do many chemicals, the characteristics of which are often unknown to the crews of the ships carrying them. There are regulations for many specified chemicals, to reduce the risk, but so many are shipped under a trade name rather than a chemical formula that they are not always identified; and new chemicals appear every year.

Already there has been an escape of chemicals which killed all the fish in the lower reaches of the Rhine, and an accumulation of mercury off Japan which affected first the fish and then the people who ate the fish, so that a number died. In an attempt to salve a sunken ship off the north coast of Spain, chemicals from her cargo were released into the sea. It was alleged that the local fisheries were virtually destroyed, and a vast claim was made. I wondered, when I heard of it, if this was another case of a political view of the matter magnifying the incident, for it occurred almost within sight of the summer home of the late General Franco.

Other reports suggest almost total pollution of Lake Erie, arising out of excessive amounts of fertilizers from surrounding farmland being washed into this vast lake by rain, and the possibility that the Baltic and Mediterranean Seas could become stinking, sterile areas deprived of all marine life. Oil, raw sewage from cities, and industrial waste are all considered to contribute to these potential disasters.

There are two aspects of this problem, the immediate risk to the life and health of people directly involved, and the long-term one of damage to the human environment. The latter can only be tackled intelligently after extensive scientific experiments, and international consideration of what is needed. In this, as in many other fields, scientific progress is less than it might be, because of a short-term and materialistic view of which scientific studies should be pursued. The question which is so often asked is : 'Will it pay?,' and it does not seem to me to matter much whether it is a question of money-making, as is so often the case in America and Europe, or a question of forwarding a materialist ideology (or, as some regard it, empire-building) as in Russia and China. A very large proportion of today's research is undertaken with these aims in mind. Could not both aims be subordinated to the far more basic and important one of 'What is necessary for man's survival?' Surely this issue must rank before experiments (with dogs and other means) to find ways to preserve the smoking habit without the present degree of risk of lung cancer, or those parts of the space programme which are purely competitive between

East and West, or the stockpiling of nuclear weapons to an extent many times greater than what would be required to destroy all life on earth.

A proper study of the sea, of what we are doing to it, and of how we can best preserve and develop its powers and productiveness, seems to me to be a priority for the United Nations. It could also produce a new driving force in education, if students and university staff (who do a great deal of research alongside or in the course of their teaching) could be encouraged to do more in this particular field. In fact, it could be promoted in all sorts of ways.

A year or two ago Geoffrey Lean, a journalist on the staff of England's celebrated regional daily newspaper *The Yorkshire Post*, was runner-up for the award for the best young journalist of the year. His main achievement at that date was a series of articles in the paper, based on careful research, on the pollution of Yorkshire rivers by chemicals and industrial waste. He named the commercial firms and nationalized industries involved, a thing which called for some courage from both him and his newspaper. I think that nearly twenty large concerns were named; and within a year or so almost all of them had taken remedial steps for abuses which in some cases had gone on for fifty or a hundred years. Since then, he has done further valuable work on the subject.

In the lower Thames, fish can now be caught again, after decades in which pollution made it impossible for a fish to live. There is talk of re-stocking it with trout and salmon.

It is not inevitable that rivers and seas should be polluted. Much has already been done by official bodies and private interests to reduce it. Much more must be done. Three things are required—first the will to do what has to be done, then the scientific information to show precisely what needs doing, and then the practical means to make action effective. The will to do it must come first.

16

What Fuel for the Future?

Oil may be said to dominate the fuel situation in the last quarter of the twentieth century. Virtually all ships are driven by it. Ashore, it produces much of our electricity, and propels most surface transport, as well as that in the air. Coal, nuclear energy, even peat still have a big part. Wood burns on many hearths, and in Asia and Africa the villagers still cook on fires of dried cow dung. But oil is king, convenient, portable, and in ample supply. But how long will it be in ample supply? Some say twenty years, some say a hundred,—not long enough in terms of human history.

The energy supply is basic for an industrialized planet. In *The Shape of Things to Come*, H.G. Wells prophesied a world currency based on a unit of energy. Whether or not he was right, energy is as basic as that.

In that remarkable book *Only One Earth*, written by Barbara Ward and René Dubos after the great United Nations conference on the environment, much space is given to the energy question. The answer to that question affects drastically both how long the world's resources will last, and whether the world will be comfortably habitable while they do last. *Only One Earth* was written before the oil-producing states raised prices and spoke of limiting production, and the resulting drop of some twenty per cent in oil consumption. However, its warnings of the dangers of the violently escalating consumption of fossil fuels are still valid. We may not know the full extent of the reserves, of which much may be beneath the sea, but they are certainly finite. No fresh supplies of oil and coal are being laid down to replace those buried so many years ago.

The two authors warned also of the effect of fuel policies on

L

man's environment generally. 'Clean air' statutes have made our cities look cleaner and put an end to London's famous 'pea-souper' fogs, which have figured in so many novels of mystery. The pollution still present in city air is dangerous in other ways. The 'smog' of Los Angeles is well-known. Living in central London as I do, I know what it is to gasp for breath on a still overcast day, when traffic fumes can neither rise through the clouds nor be blown away by the wind. Experts in such places as the Victoria and Albert Museum say that chemicals in the air (mostly sulphur dioxide from sulphur in fuel) have done more damage in the last decade to old stone and antique fabrics than all the hazards of hundreds of years. Recently, the Greek authorities were proposing to encase the remaining sculptures on the Parthenon in airtight cases before they were destroyed entirely by the same cause.

Nuclear-fuelled power stations are still multiplying. They bring with them unsolved problems in connection with radioactive and toxic materials, especially in the disposal of waste. No way is yet known of making this safe. Its horrifying dangers can be confined for a period by skilful storage. We leave a real solution, if there is one, to our descendants, to whom we bequeath quantities of dangerous material which increase month by month. Should we do this?

On any grounds, economic or ecological, it seems to me that far more attention should be paid to developing different sources of power, sources which would be big enough for the expanding population, and which would not have the damaging effect on our surroundings of coal, oil, or nuclear power. Hydro-electric power is the cleanest major source in use at present; but the taming of rivers and waterfalls for this purpose can produce a hastening of our rush towards a wholly artificial environment.

Tidal power has been suggested. To harness it on a large scale would deeply affect the balance of nature in many tidal areas. It might, for example, hamper the development of fish upon which we shall increasingly rely for food as the population grows. I think it was Olaf Stapledon in *Last and First Men* who predicted that a large scale harnessing of tides would ultimately slow down the rotation of the earth. Perhaps he over-estimated the risk, but this would be another quite incalculable interference with man's environment. Wind-power and the interesting British proposal to harness the wave-power of the North Atlantic by a raft several miles long would not basically affect the equation of our energy needs and supplies.

The new power source will have to be enormous. Today, more than half the merchant tonnage afloat consists of oil tankers. The individual ships, too, have grown larger than was once considered possible. My own first comment on a 'very large crude carrier' (the crude refers to the oil and not the ship) was, 'It looks like Southend Pier going to sea.' And after that came the 'ultra-large crude carrier'.

These great ships, carrying 100,000, 200,000, 300,000 or more tons, brought in a completely new range of technology. Their construction speeded up the development of pre-fabrication and many other changes in shipyard processes. Their navigation, with the difficulties of stopping or changing direction of a mass with such enormous momentum, made the old rules of navigation out of date. There actually had to be changes made in the rules to prevent collisions at sea. Their crews are often less in number than those of smaller ships, due to automated engine controls. Some say that they are not seamen any more, only button pressers and switch pullers. And if something goes wrong, a leak or a fire, the scale of the trouble is so huge that the handful of men on board can do little about it.

In the summer of 1975, by courtesy of Ingénieur-Général Yves Rocquemont, I had the privilege of being shown the work in progress at Cap d'Antifer, near Le Havre, and to see how the logical French were tackling the supply of fuel to an oil-based industry. They were building a completely new port, and simul-taneously building at St Nazaire the ships to use it. At Antifer, the new breakwater, then nearly complete, would shelter a jetty with deep-water berths where two 550,000-ton ships could lie alongside. Pipelines would carry the crude oil to no less than nine refineries in France and Belgium.

Even the construction of the port involved completely new techniques. Concrete was being made on the beach with limestone from the adjoining cliffs and sand dredged out of the sea, the two being mixed with sea-water. I thought you could not make cement set with sea-water, but the French found a way. And the work was going forward at amazing speed. The port was operational by the end of that year.

The conception was new, the techniques were new; and, even in the context of the rapidly changing world situation on oil, it was plain that the Antifer plan would be a valuable asset for the next twenty years.

Many other new techniques have been developed : the 'load-on-top' procedure to make it unnecessary to dispose of the drainings from washed tanks and thus risk pollution; the offshore loading terminals where ships too big to come inshore take their oil at buoys from submerged pipelines; and trans-shipment both at sea and in port, whereby the big tankers of yesterday become the small 'feeder-ships' of today, to distribute the cargoes from their bigger and younger sisters.

The size of the oil operation causes even the mistakes in it to shake the affairs of the world. Accidents to large tankers in the Malacca Strait threatened pollution of the coasts of Singapore, Indonesia and Malaysia. The Strait is narrow. Standing on the beach in Singapore, I could see the lights across the Strait only eight miles away. The waters are relatively shallow, too, and rocky. Yet through here go the hundreds of tankers to and from the Persian Gulf, to supply the oil-based economy of Japan. Thus when there was talk of closing the Strait to the big tankers, there was dismay in Japan. Even the addition of a day or two to each voyage by sending the ships round Sumatra would make a difference to the standard of living in Japan.

A more dramatic example was the unexpected reduction of oil consumption in 1975. It came at a time of rapid increase of tanker-building, supported enthusiastically by shipowners, shipbuilders (who had expanded their operations enormously), banks (eager to advance money for mortgages), and governments (equally eager that employment should be available for their citizens). A slump of unprecedented size hit the tanker freight market. Rows of laid-up ships appeared in Norway, in Greece, in England.

At the same time new ships were being delivered without any prospect of cargoes. When the 275,000-ton *Olympic Bravery* went on the rocks near Brest, she was on her maiden voyage—to a lying-up berth in Norway. Some of the biggest shipowners found themselves unable to meet their obligations to pay the instalments on their ships. They owed so much to the banks that to avoid even greater losses the banks agreed to postpone payments of sums due to them.

Cancellation of orders for ships pending became commonplace. One group alone, Maritime Fruit Carriers, cancelled orders for ships amounting to 10 per cent of the entire tonnage then on order from the British shipbuilding industry. Meanwhile, Japanese shipyards, to keep going, cut their prices by from 25 to 40 per cent.

The organization of independent owners of tankers, Intertanko, called an international conference of shipowers, shipbuilders, oil companies and banks, with a view to joint action. A press report said that shipowners' aggregate debts to the banks for new tonnage amounted to $135,000m. How that figure was arrived at, I have no idea, but the real total was certainly colossal. A view I heard expressed was that the situation could only be remedied by a moratorium on orders for new ships, and by reduction of the world's shipbuilding capacity by half. If this were done, it would have major economic, social and political consequences. In Northern Ireland, for example, Harland and Wolff's shipyard has been the biggest single industrial employer. If those thousands of men were to be thrown out of work, what effect would it have on the already high unemployment, and on the level of political violence, somewhat damped down at that point though it was?

These things indicate the scale of the energy issue. It is, too, at the heart of every country's desire for economic progress. We need new sources of power, even more liberal than those available today, and if possible without the disadvantage of polluting the environment, as with coal, oil and nuclear power.

The tapping of the heat of the earth's core is one means which has been suggested to provide power for the future. To me, it does not appeal, for once again, we would be embarking on a course the end of which no man can foresee. Scientists say that the heat supply is so vast that the proportion which would be withdrawn would be minute, and the possible side-effects hardly capable of measurement. But suppose they are wrong. Suppose it meant, in the end, a five-degree lowering of the temperature of air and sea all over the world? It would be a catastrophe.

The energy source I would bank on for the future is the sun. Active research is proceeding now on how to harness all that light and heat (so much more than we need in some latitudes) for various uses—domestic water and space heating and lighting, chiefly. At present, although some solar energy is being harnessed, the process is not efficient. Nor was the first steam engine. I feel certain that sufficient research and experiment in the next few decades could put this lovely stuff to work—and do no harm by pollution to anything at all.

Such an achievement would have an interesting by-product. In general, sunlight is most plentiful in those parts of the earth where people are poorest. If sunlight becomes wealth, this could restore some of the balance between the tropics and the temperate zones. (Some consider that the prosperity of countries in the temperate zones is caused by the inhabitants being encouraged by the climate to work harder. Others choose a different cause—the nagging influence of the Puritan conscience to prod people into more activity!)

Presumably, the power into which sunlight will be converted will mostly be in the form of hot water or of electricity. The technique of harnessing heat-exchange in liquids is already well understood, but for power which has to be distributed, an electrical form would be convenient.

The major problem, once we have more efficient ways of harnessing the power, will be that of transporting it to the points where it is used. At present, it is difficult to apply electric power to road, sea and air vehicles, compared with the easy portability of oil products. Far better batteries or accumulators will be required if ships, planes, and cars are to be run by electricity from solar sources, but many feel that such a development is already overdue.

Parallel with development of the new power source, another big improvement is also overdue—a campaign against the present waste of energy resources. The automobile of today is about twenty per cent efficient. The other eighty per cent of the power produced by the engine is mostly radiated into the car's immediate neighbourhood with no advantage except to keep the engine at a working temperature. An American oil man told me oil has been so cheap in his country that no one tried to insulate a factory against heat loss in winter. It was cheaper to burn the oil and let most of the heat escape than to design and erect a building which was itself efficient. And for this we have been burning up our limited stock of fossil fuels.

Many people have admired the achievement of the British farming industry. Its productivity in the last quarter-century has increased much more than any other major British industry. A farmer friend in Dorset, jointly with some neighbours, bought a harvesting machine from a highly developed European country, and found that it could not cope with the weight of crop produced by British fields. However, experts say that this progress has been bought by (among other things) a lavish squandering of cheap oil and electrical power, indoors and out. The net gain, therefore, is small.

Again, the cooling towers of many electricity power stations fail to use something like three-fifths of the heat produced in the process, and discharge it into rivers and seas, to the surprise and sometimes delight of the fish. But what a waste!

When I was a young man, I used to predict that men would be on the moon in my life-time. Will I live long enough to see sleek ships driven by solar-generated electric power surging across or under the seas, silent, odourless, and pollution-free?

17

Retirement

Retirement strikes different people in many different ways. Some seem to die almost at once. One day, they have a status and a familiar function; the next, their reason for living seems to have vanished. One day, they have a reasonable income; the next, a much less comfortable pension. One day, they have a familiar routine, tasks to carry out which they know and understand, the equipment, facilities and colleagues required to fulfil those tasks; the next, the framework has disappeared. The change is too much for them. In a few weeks, months or years, the mechanism runs down, vitality seeps out of their system, life comes to an untimely end.

I used to think that schoolmasters were particularly prone to this. In the years after I left Christ's Hospital, I seemed to see frequent reports of my old masters dying soon after their retirement. I wondered if, lacking the continuing stimulus of contact with wave after wave of new young people, and all their freshness, challenge, and irritating faults, life could not go on for the guides and teachers of youth. But this is not the problem of one profession only.

Some retired people, on the other hand, get busier than ever. A phrase I hear with a frequency which seems more and more boring and unreal is, 'I'm so busy since I retired that I wonder how I found the time to go to work.' Many sincerely believe it is true. Others pretend so. They bustle around, filling every minute with activity, regardless of whether it is significant or not.

There are many other variations. Christopher Hayman, a City accountant who retired a little early because of ill health, told me that he had taken seriously to the piano, practising several hours a day, and sitting in sequence the examinations of increasing difficulty, the first of which are the terror of so many small boys and girls. The insurance manager of an oil company, a proper Cockney, married to a girl from a remote Welsh village, retired with her, after his London career ended, to her tiny village. A friend told me that he revelled in it, was elected to the local council, and took part in everything. His wife, however, was bored stiff !

Most people have to retire nowadays. The rules force them to give up the work which, whether they loved it or hated it, occupied most of their waking hours for most of their years. At 65 or 70, often at 60, sometimes even at 55, the axe falls. Usually there is no choice about it, although some want to work on and some don't, some are at their best when they have to give up, and some are physically and mentally ready for it even earlier.

A few months after I retired, a former colleague asked me how I was finding life. I said that I had found the adjustment difficult. 'I'm glad you said that,' he replied, paused, and added : 'I wouldn't have believed you if you had said you did not.'

When I embarked upon retirement on 1st January 1973, I had (as is shown in Chapter 1 of this book) two priceless assets, a long experience of a varied and fascinating form of business, and a conviction, reinforced over many years, that there was an ideal plan for each person's life, both in general and in every detail. There were other great assets, too. One was a wife who had stuck with me through good and ill for forty years, who patiently battled with my weaknesses (usually with patience, anyway), and who encouraged me to aim at the best.

Then, too, we had enough money to give us a reasonable freedom of action. My firm was generous in its pension arrangements, not just to me, but to all. We had little capital, but a fairly good income.

Still more important, our general health was good. Not long before, all the senior people in the firm had been given a detailed medical check, and I had paid for a similar one for my wife. Both of us had escaped serious illness or disability. My only real defects were the slow deterioration in eyesight and a little arthritis.

One might say, therefore, that a world of choices was open to us.

What sort of a world was it to choose in ? If it was a question

of problems which needed answers, there was a wide range—
violence of many kinds in many countries, corruption in high
places in the U.S.A. and in our own country and elsewhere,
children often leaving school uneducated, industry failing to meet
the needs of millions, the rapid exhaustion of some raw materials,
the space exploration programme bogged down, industrial blight
spreading ashore and at sea, the increasing gap between the
wealth of some countries and the poverty of others.

On the other hand, there were many hopeful signs. Changes
were brewing in industry, in the direction of better training, of
more consultation with and participation by all types of personnel. International co-operation was (to a degree) increasing. The
United States was offering a hand to Russia and to China. Britain
was probably heading for membership of the European Economic
Community. The United Nations was interesting itself in the
whole basic issue of man's environment.

On a level which I found easier to grasp, the force of Moral
Re-Armament was involved in all these issues, through men and
women (many of whom we knew) in various parts of the world.
Some were in industry and business, including employers pioneer-
ing new approaches, and workers who had turned from barren
class-war attitudes to a greater and more positive militancy for
the good of all. Some of them, for example, had helped in creating
a new teamwork between the French and British and some other
European aerospace industries.

As regards violence and acute political problems, I knew of
more than one instance where the change in men which Moral
Re-Armament promotes had resulted in solutions to what could,
in each case, have become a full-scale civil war. One concerned
the quarter-million German-speaking minority in northern Italy,
the Alto Adige or South Tyrol, transferred from Austria to Italy
in 1919. Ever since, the authorities had tried to integrate them
fully into Italy, and they had resisted by all means, including
guns and bombs. At a conference at the M.R.A. centre in Switzerland, I had heard their leaders speak of the first steps towards a
settlement, and by 1973 there was talk of an amendment to the
Italian constitution to ratify the final agreement.

Nearer home, Northern Ireland was still locked in a bitter
struggle, although our own most recent visit to see Unionist and

Republican friends had convinced us that many were turning away from violence. Prime Minister Edward Heath, asked in a B.B.C. Radio interview if he thought there was any possibility of a settlement, said stoutly : 'Of course there is', and added that, if the Italians could solve the issue of the Alto Adige, Britain could do the same in Northern Ireland.

The world-wide action of Moral Re-Armament is very hard to describe or define. For one thing, it changes constantly. 'The Spirit bloweth where it listeth'. Sometimes it is very public and on a mass scale, sometimes quiet, private, man to man, woman to woman. The two main factors in it are, first, a small army of individuals in all kinds of jobs and homes in many countries, living their lives in the same surroundings as everyone else, but concerned to bring a change for the better around them; and second, a number who are free to travel or to stay anywhere, who are as independent as possible from other commitments, so that they can help the first group to be fully effective. These, who are carefully vetted and trained for the task, work without salary, relying entirely on what they may have or (more likely) what others may be moved to give them for their needs.

A question which many of my friends ask is, 'Who is the leader of Moral Re-Armament?' It was of course started by an American, Dr Frank Buchman, but he battled for all the rest of his life to avoid being its leader, and to encourage all and sundry to take initiative and leadership. When he died, the English writer-sportsman-farmer Peter Howard became the most conspicuous figure, through his remarkable commitment and abilities. Like Buchman, he strove to bring others forward. Like Buchman, he had some but not complete success. Since Howard's death in 1965, there has in fact been no individual leader in theory or fact. I know many of the most responsible people in it, but would be hard put to it to grade them in any way. It is a collective leadership, a true democracy, a real world family, where in principle every person tries to develop others.

All kinds of methods are used to spread M.R.A.'s ideas—plays, films, books, meetings, conferences, all the mass media from time to time; but the basic ingredient is personal touch. Certainly, what has affected me most is this contact with loyal and dedicated people.

Would this work, or some aspect of it, fill my life after I finished with a full-time paid job? This was, however, the wrong question. For a long time past, my life had been permeated with M.R.A., at least to a degree. To give but one example, I had dealt with an accident in Nigerian waters, just before that country gained her independence. A British ship, moored at buoys, broke adrift and hit a jetty, damaging the jetty and suffering damage herself. The cost of repairs was a few thousand pounds. Enquiry showed that the sole cause of the accident was the bad upkeep of the moorings, which were government-owned. Lawyers told us that an action for damages against the new independent government of Nigeria would succeed. They had taken over both the assets and the liabilities of the colony.

I thought about the situation quite a bit. Then I wrote to the shipowners and to the insurers of the ship, reported how matters stood, and added that it would not, perhaps, be the best thing for the new country to be sued for damages because of the faults of the earlier colonial administration. What did they think? Both parties cordially agreed. Lloyd's and the insurance companies paid for the damage to the ship. My firm paid for the damage to the jetty. My own view is that this was an example of 'moral re-armament' in all concerned. Not, perhaps, a very remarkable instance, but a proper one.

However, if one decides to take one's part in this programme fully, it does involve more than action by (as in the words of the hymn) 'you in your small corner, and I in mine'. Co-ordination of initiative is essential. It may be informal, but it is often on a large scale. For example, the Swiss have sponsored major conferences, open to all nations, each year for thirty years.

On the other hand, a move by anyone can develop into something much bigger. In 1940 Dick Haile, a photographer in Bognor Regis, Sussex, had certain thoughts about civilian response to national needs in wartime. They dealt with rumours, food rationing, industrial production, and so on, and he set them out on a card headed in large type 'MORALE'. In a matter of months, the card was reproduced and issued in millions of copies throughout Britain, particularly by civic authorities, including the Lord Mayors and Lord Provosts of most of the big cities. It recalled people under stress to the eternal moral and spiritual values, and obviously met a genuine need.

In 1975, a handful of trade unionists issued a national appeal called 'Action 75', arising from Prime Minister Wilson's suggestion to the miners to 'give a year to Britain'. It drew enthusiastic support from such well-known figures as Graham Hill, the racing driver, and Group-Captain Douglas Bader. A piquant factor was that the chairman of the organizing committee, Albert Ingram, a worker in British Leyland Motors, had played a very different part a few years earlier, before he began to apply M.R.A. principles. A leading figure in what was sometimes called the 'Broad Left', he had attacked and helped to wreck the industrial policy of an earlier Wilson administration.

It was two housewives in Herefordshire who, again in 1975, set out to put more positive content into International Women's Year. Their moves snowballed to include a big meeting in London's Royal Festival Hall, a speech at the main world conference of International Women's Year in Mexico City, and action in Australia and New Zealand.

Similarly, ordinary citizens affected by M.R.A. have initiated big public moves in other countries; journalists and students in India, dockers in Brazil, a schoolmaster in Sweden.

Would my wife and I find, in the release from my regular work, occupation in this world programme? Again, it was the wrong question.

But what was the right one? What is in fact the task of the individual? I suppose that it is to help to bring about the right changes in the world, and in this task one's greatest asset may be one's touches with people, the web which holds the world together. The individual's task, like the overall programme, is difficult to define, and may change constantly.

We spent time, as is our regular practice, in seeking guidance, and we only developed two simple points upon which we were both convinced. The first was that we should keep on our flat in central London, and not retire to some quiet village or care-free island. The second was that we should keep in touch, as far as possible, with the world of business and industry.

Two other things had already developed, which helped to shape our immediate future. My firm had asked me to continue to act as technical adviser to an international body concerned with merchant ships. This meant about three conferences of a few days each, every year, and some work in between. And I had started writing *Ships That Go Bump in the Night*.

Several friends had suggested that I should write some account of my business life. There is very little in print about this kind of business. What there is, is highly technical, and would be baffling to the general reader. The idea appealed to me more and more, as I thought about it. After all, I had enjoyed the life. It could well be that others would enjoy reading about it. Moreover, it might be possible to explode a few misconceptions, and put forward some positive ideas for consideration.

Many people ask me how long it took to write. The first draft took four months. It was set down in longhand, and mostly straight off the top of my mind. Then another eight months were occupied in revision and in finding a publisher. Writing the first draft was great fun; the second stage was interesting, but rather a grind. Perhaps the reason for this was that I knew almost nothing at all about publishing, the hard facts of which had to be learned by trial and error.

The contract was signed just about a year after I first put pen to paper, and naturally there was still a good deal of work before the book actually came out. Altogether, the project took a good deal of my time in the first two years after retirement.

Then, there was the immediate family. Our son and daughter were well established, both married, and each with two children : Brian a chartered accountant, working in the electrical industry; Veronica married to a patent agent, and herself working as a technical translator with a small office near the Law Courts. Since they lived within an hour's drive, one north, the other south, it was good to be reasonably often in touch with them and their growing children.

Another advantage of our staying on in our conveniently situated flat was that it was easier for our friends in other countries to drop in to see us. Within days of my retirement, two Yugoslavs did this. Our visitors' book gives further evidence in the months that followed. There is the name of my nephew from Brussels, then two Greek shipowners and their wives, the secretary who helped to type my book and her husband, a merchant navy cap-

tain, a nuclear physicist just home from lecturing in Israel, a
senior French civil servant I had met in my work, one of my
management trainees from my firm with his wife, and a New
Zealand couple we met on a cruising holiday round the Greek
islands. India and Australia were represented, too, a senior couple
from Rhodesia, a judge and several others from Cyprus.

We found, too, that visits to other countries were not difficult,
and to many parts of our own. In the first three years, for different
reasons and varying periods, we visited eleven countries.

Early in 1976 came the new challenge, the invitation from my
former partners to go back to the City one day a week.

I had certain other responsibilities, too. I was chairman of two
charitable trusts; and when a residents' association was formed
for the 182 flats in our two blocks, I served as chairman of that
for the first two years.

Thus, there was an ample range of activity for me, and I could
easily have filled my waking hours with this task and that. The
aspect which concerned me, all the time, was not occupation, but
whether I was doing the right things for the right reasons and in
the right way. In youth, one feels one's future to be limitless—all
the time in the world, and the days and years pass almost imper-
ceptibly. In middle life, time seems to have accelerated. One
wants to do more than there is time to do. And as the time ahead
shortens, so does it seem more important, not less, to use it well.

This may account, in part, for my finding readjustment difficult, for the unease which still at times attacks me, and makes
me ask if I am doing the right things. To work with a given framework, as one does in a paid job, is a different thing from con-
structing a way of life without those guide-lines.

A second reason may be linked to the issue which so many think
is significant in industry today, the issue of 'job satisfaction'. Some
put so much importance on it that they attack some of the most
basic elements in today's large-scale industry. They would abolish
the assembly line. They would like to turn back, to a large extent,
the whole process of mechanization.

I can sympathize with the idea, although I do not accept it
fully.

On the one hand, I think of the visit my wife and I once paid
to the little village of Kersey in Suffolk. There is just one street,

which tips down a hill, splashes through a stream at the bottom, and climbs again the other side. Halfway down the hill from the ornate church which tops one crest there is a cluster of buildings in rosy red brick. Here lives and works a potter. He specializes in plain, heavy ware, fired at a high temperature, and does all the work and even the selling himself. We looked over the display, and bought a piece or two. I asked if business was good. He replied : 'Good enough. And I wake every morning to know that I will spend the day doing the things I love to do.'

On the other hand, I recall an impromptu talk given at a private dinner by the director of personnel research of one of the great British motor companies. He spoke of the scores of thousands of workers, many of whom repeat endlessly a two-and-a-half minute 'slug' of work as the cars pass along the assembly line. Some, he admitted, chafe against it, but many like to have their work organized that way. Of those who do, some are extremely creative in their spare time in all kinds of crafts, wood and metal work, the breeding of animals and birds, and so on. He thought it impossible to make simple rules as to what industrial systems were suitable to individuals, and what were not. People vary so much.

One way or another, I feel sure that 'job satisfaction' is a worthy aim for everyone, and so is 'retirement satisfaction'. Sometimes, the system should be adjusted for the sake of the people most involved; sometimes we must (at least temporarily) adjust ourselves to the system.

Some years ago, I read of a worker in a Scottish factory making tractors. He had been a real trouble-maker, and it was a minor sensation when he was found to be no longer causing tension, disputes and strikes in his section. When asked why, he said that he had begun to understand what the tractors they produced meant in terms of extra food to some of the poorer countries they supplied, and this had given a new meaning to his work.

This seems to hit a very important note. We all need to feel useful, that we matter to other people, that we have a contribution to make. And it is a greater quality if we can help others to this experience. Perhaps this is what, most of all, I have been seeking in retirement, a way to help others to adjust themselves to life, to find in their own way the sense of purpose which has been so vital a factor to me personally ever since 1933. The trouble is,

I suppose, that basically I am a very selfish person, and it is a constant effort to think for others, to try to understand their different viewpoints, and to do what will help them in some way or other. For me, this is perhaps the greatest value of that time of listening each morning. It rarely fails to include something to prod me in the direction of doing something for someone else.

The year 1975 certainly included the most eye-opening experience my wife and I had had since retirement, a six weeks' tour of North America. It came about through a convergence of several influences.

My book *Ships That Go Bump in the Night* had been published, and I had received a number of letters from business friends who wanted copies, and a few from people who had read it, and commented on various aspects of it. Many of these were from the U.S.A., and some urged me and my wife to visit them.

In the previous couple of years the United States had gone through the purgatory of the Watergate enquiry, which had shaken deeply the belief of its people in its most treasured democratic institutions. On top of this had come the collapse of U.S. policy in South-East Asia, and the country's total withdrawal from Vietnam, Cambodia and Laos, and almost simultaneously an economic recession, with a great surge in unemployment. Constance and I felt enormous sympathy for our American friends. Their country had been pursued with such abuse by certain elements, that they were bruised and shaken, even before these successive blows of disgrace, failure and hardship.

We felt a strong urge to be with our friends at a time when they needed encouragement. There was not, perhaps, much which one couple could do, but (as a friend in Houston, Texas, said to us later) 'it's the total of what we all do which counts'.

The third aspect was that the work of Moral Re-Armament in the United States and Canada, after some difficulties, was moving ahead strongly. We would be glad to help with this, if we could, and just as we were nearing a point of decision, we were invited to a North American conference for M.R.A. in Banff, Alberta, at a time which fitted well with our tentative plans.

Would it be possible to weave all these elements together into a reasonable pattern? We had been consulting various people in North America and Britain, and it appeared that it could be done.

M

The most important factor was an American couple, Richard and Randolph Ruffin. We had known them in England before and after their marriage; and in November 1971 when Dick was a U.S. Navy officer attached to the Pentagon, they had entertained me in the apartment they then had in Alexandria, Virginia. (I had been asked to Washington to confer with certain government bodies on aspects of maritime law.) Since then, Dick had refused an offer of a senior planning post in the Pentagon, so that they could both work without salary for Moral Re-Armament in their own country or elsewhere, as needs arose. They were a responsible and sensitive couple, much younger than us, of course, and we respected their knowledge and commitment.

We were also very conscious of our own limited knowledge of their country. Our previous visits had been brief, either to attend a specific conference, or a flying trip on business to New York or Washington. The last, just before I retired in 1972, was for a week in New York, when I saw, I think, all the principal firms carrying containers by sea, and introduced a younger partner to those of them he did not know already. A visit of that sort, crowded with interviews on a narrow technical range, and confined to one port, gives a very inaccurate impression of such a vast and complex country.

We sent the Ruffins full details of what we particularly wanted to do, and what else we would be glad to do if we could, and in due course got a reply from Dick which said : 'I am strongly inclined to feed all your information into the big computer at the Pentagon, but somehow. . . .' In short, they would meet us in New York with a car, and would travel with us at least for the first part of the journey; and we would plan it together.

So began a journey through nine states and the District of Columbia, and right across Canada, much of it by car. This is not a travel book, so I will simply say that the whole point of the thing became clearer and clearer as we went on. It was all built round people. We soon decided that, if it was to be a choice between sight-seeing and seeing people, it was people all the time.

We saw a few sights, of course, Washington Irving's home at Sleepy Hollow, Independence Hall in Philadelphia, and the aerospace collection in Washington, with the Wright brothers' aeroplane, Lindbergh's 'Spirit of St Louis', and the Apollo moon capsule all in the same room. We saw skyscrapers and prairies, countless motorways and equally immeasurable Atlantic beaches, but the people were the great fascination.

It was interesting to see how even the speech changed as we moved south. I was charmed when, in Virginia, we were first addressed as 'you-all', but in Texas it seemed to become 'y'all'. And I shall not soon forget the Southern belle, all creamy skin, great dark eyes and raven hair, who sat next to me at dinner in New Orleans, and drawled, 'Ah come from Miss'sippi.'

We were almost drowned in kindness. What they say about American hospitality is true, twice over. But there was with it a thoughtful consideration for people no longer very young who might not want to hustle, and this made everything even more enjoyable.

By stages, and often by road, we travelled from New York right round to Texas. The Ruffins met our business friends, their wives and their associates, to a number of 80 or 90 or so, and we met the Ruffins' friends and relations, another hundred or more. Both come from old Virginia families. Dick is a direct descendant of that Edmund S. Ruffin who fired the first shot at Fort Sumter in the war between the States. His wife, a Randolph on her mother's side, is daughter of the principal of The High School, and brought up on its campus. (To a Virginian, his state's attractions include what he invariably calls The University, The Country Club and The High School.) Their friends, however, were by no means limited to Virginia, or to the old families. Through them we met, for example, two black leaders of the longshoremen, a celebrated opera singer, some of the youth, and the chairman of a great corporation who (to judge by the big game trophies which decorated his office) thoroughly merited the description of tycoon.

Our own friends were mostly in the ports, many of them maritime lawyers. One had become a federal judge, another a high official in Washington. We also knew one of the ambassadors there; and in New York we had the pleasure and privilege of staying some days with one of the British ministers to the United Nations, as well as with two of our generous legal friends.

In one city, where four of our lawyer friends entertained us to lunch, Dick told them how shocked he had been, visiting a famous law school, to hear that most of the undergraduates scoffed at legal ethics, and treated their training as being for one purpose only—to learn how to manipulate the system in favour of their clients. The four exploded with indignation, one saying: 'It's true. We've met some of these men, and we won't have them in our office.' I had a similar reaction in Galveston, Texas, where the lawyer in question added, 'We will have nothing to do with this philosophy. We know that some in our profession have accepted a debasing of standards, but we have not. And we think this is partly due to our association over many years with clients who have high principles, particularly firms like yours, and Lloyd's.' It was a humbling thought. It also reminded one that President Nixon himself, Vice-President Agnew, and most of the defendants in the Watergate trials had been practising lawyers.

Our overall impression was that the United States was recovering from the reverses of the previous years, an impression which was strengthened in the following months by improvements in American trade and employment figures. This was hardly surprising with such a young and buoyant country. Its resources in men, technology, raw materials and all that makes wealth, are vast, and it is bound to have a giant future unless the country's spirit fails. It had faltered, but the cross-section of people we saw certainly gave the impression that they were beginning to bounce back.

From shipowner and docker, tycoon and trade union official, we got some interesting side-lights on industrial matters. A trade union news sheet to its members listed strikes in progress at the time of going to press, rather like a sports report. (The body in question was said to be communist-dominated.) In the spacious entry hall of Reynolds Metals' great head office in Richmond, Virginia, there were canisters into which staff could throw aluminium soft-drink cans and such, for re-cycling. The company had just negotiated fresh agreements giving Jamaica a high price for bauxite. The pump attendant at a filling station complained of the high price of gasoline. I did a mental calculation, and told him that in England it was nearly three times his price.

A feature article in the *New York Times* referred to the purchase of many square miles of prairie in the Midwest, to see if the original prairie conditions could be restored. The first settlers had found grass ten feet high, full of flowers and wild animals, and with roots that broke the blades of iron ploughs. The paper linked the restoration project interestingly with a country-wide revival of interest in handicrafts.

At Giddings, Texas, we watched for a while a small-town cattle auction. At the door a white-haired character in patched jeans and a broad-brimmed white straw hat (as worn by most of the men present) said : 'C'mon in. You'll be all right. Just give the auctioneer a nod or a wink now and then to let him know you're comfortable.' The stock, sold one by one with machine-gun rapidity in an air-conditioned barn, were gaunt from the dry weather and lack of feed, but we were told they would soon fatten up.

In the evening of that day, we were in very different surroundings, the drawing-room of Angus and Frances Springer, with the Dean of Fine Arts and other staff of South-western University, the editor of the local paper and others. Angus was professor of drama there, and we had met them in London during his sabbatical year. The evening gave several indications of the effect of ideas on society. The drama department of South-western had produced on campus several of the plays first presented professionally at the Westminster Theatre in London, and sponsored there by Moral Re-Armament. They had also recommended them to other universities.

I asked why so many students took the drama course. Did they go into the professional theatre? Very few, was the reply. The attraction was the experience it gave of working with a team, and the combination for a single purpose of a number of varied skills—direction, acting, painting, costume, electronics, finance, and so on.

Two days later, we were in a plane flying from Dallas (where they say that some air-condition their patios and barbecue pits, as well as their houses!) to Vancouver. Here again we met a wide range of people, especially in industry, and again including a number of business friends. Two quite senior lawyers there, one the son of a cabinet minister, the other the son of a judge, had been students in our London office twenty years before, and we had kept in touch ever since.

Another couple we met, quite new friends, were also going to the conference we planned to attend in Banff, and invited us to go with them by car. It was over 400 miles, right through the mountains—a generous offer, which was eagerly accepted. And our expectations were far, far exceeded.

Canada, too, introduced us to what was for me the most impressive single element in our whole colourful journey—the North American Indians. In Vancouver and again in Banff we had the chance to meet, talk with and listen to Chiefs of several tribes. It was an education.

My reading since early youth had introduced me to several different word pictures of the Indian, the noble child of nature, the bloodthirsty killer and torturer, the drink-sodden victim of white men's exploitation, from Fenimore Cooper to Jack London, from Howard Fast to Louis L'Amour. More recently, the papers had headlined troubles on the reservations in the United States, and I knew that links existed between tribes right across the continent. Years before, at a conference on Mackinae Island, Michigan, a man closely in touch with the Indians told us that tribes as far apart as Canada and California knew of the island's special association with the Great Spirit, Gitche Manito, first encountered by me in Longfellow's *Hiawatha*. My instinct was that there was an element of truth in all the different stories of the red man, but none probably held the whole truth.

The first chief we met, in British Columbia, had set himself to revive the old crafts of his people, and to this end had established a store where the work could be exhibited and sold. He showed us a half-completed totem pole which had been commissioned from his carvers, a great cedar log, and told us how each pole was modelled to tell a story, beginning from the top. A memorial pole, for example, told the story of the dead man's life. Four basic colours were used, blue representing the sky, green for the forest, red for the earth, and black for the sea.

As he spoke of the history of his people, his very voice seemed to change, and the listeners seemed to be carried into a new dimension, where the past and the present were one. Times long ago were as immediate and vivid as what was happening now. The fish and the whales, to these dwellers by the sea, were personalities.

So, too, with the tribes from the mountains and prairies, whom we met in Banff. To them, animals and people, streams, mountains, the eagles and the tall trees were all part with each other in a living unity. One chief compared the peoples of the world to the trees, which are of many colours, but together make a beautiful forest. They were realistic about their own people's failings, the idleness and drunkenness which had followed upon their living as government pensioners on their reservations. More important, most of their leaders are encouraging an independence of mind which promotes self-reliance and economic independence, too, a revival of their pride in their heritage.

One of our Vancouver lawyer friends had acted for a coastal tribe which had been reduced to a condition of 93 per cent unemployment, and was degenerating hopelessly. Its leadership decided to fight back against the trend, and to establish a fish cannery. The men caught the fish, the women packed them. The government loan for construction of the plant had been paid off. With other activities, almost the whole tribe had found work, and recovered their self-respect.

Coming through the mountains, our Canadian host, a retired government official, showed us an Indian reserve where the tribe, among other occupations, were responsible for the deer herds in the area. They never over-hunted or under-hunted a herd, he said. They never killed just for sport, or cut off a meal and left the corpse to rot. When they killed, they used every part of the animal for different purposes, for they respected it as being (like themselves) a part of creation. While we were in Vancouver, a government spokesman reported consideration of a proposal to give back to the Indians of the province complete control of their own affairs.

The Indians at Banff spoke in poetic phrases, full of imagery from nature. It was strangely moving, to someone like myself, so close most of his life to city ways and high technology. One of them said that they had a recurring difficulty in living simultaneously in two cultures. I could understand that.

The greatest thing they gave, however, was their direct and warm approach to other people. At the first session, they welcomed to their land the visitors from all over Canada and the United States, and from a number of other countries. The first speaker, a chief of the Stony Indians, began with the simple words, 'Brothers and sisters'. A group of French Canadians were there,

One of them said afterwards: 'We think of ourselves as an oppressed minority, but when I heard those words, I thought of the way in which we in the past treated the Indians.'

Other minorities were represented there, including Ukrainians from Alberta, and the blacks who are now a substantial group in parts of Canada as well as in the U.S.A. But there are simple ways to bridge the gaps and solve the problems, ways which come from a simple change of attitude in men. The American Indians today are, in the main, trained in Christianity at Catholic and Protestant mission schools. They seemed to find this a fulfilment of the belief of their ancestors (who are so real and close to them) in a Great Spirit which watches over all on earth.

We went to America in the hope of doing something there for friends, old and new. I hope we succeeded. I am sure that they did a great deal for us, and we will never be quite the same again, after that experience.

Retirement is proving to be a doorway to new things for me, new thinking and new experiences. Perhaps it will be a realization, in part at least, of the dreams of youth, the dreams of a better world, of understanding between people, and a clear purpose for my own life and those of others.

18

From Man to Man

Will Rogers, America's cowboy humorist, is said to have made a statement early in the 1939-45 war on the Allies' losses of merchant ships sunk by submarines. The answer, he thought, was a simple one—just raise the temperature of the sea to boiling point. When asked how this might be done, he replied : 'I get the ideas. Someone else can work out the details.'

One wishes that this approach, of total devolution of responsibility, could be applied to every problem. But if it is a question of making dreams come true, of producing a better society which really works, most of us, like Will Rogers, are quite prepared to pontificate on the big issues, and leave the details to others.

The problem which baffles us is how change can be produced. It baffles me so often that I am reluctant even to write about it, but I will, nevertheless. It is needed.

First of all, we have to accept that the problem is a human one. There is nothing basically wrong with our circumstances, with the earth, its varied beauty and its huge resources. The wrong things are aspects of man, or of what man has made. What man has marred, man can re-make, whether it is a landscape or a relationship.

The problem, therefore, is how to change man. When I was invited to resume management training at my own firm, I was at once faced with one aspect of this. What qualities were needed in the trainees, and how could they be developed?

It is ludicrous to suggest that people do not change. A senior man in one of the multi-national oil companies said to me once, 'Anyone who thinks people cannot change should compare how folk behaved with oil at three dollars a barrel with how they behaved when it became twelve dollars a barrel.' Most of us know men and women who were quite different after marriage from what they were before. More responsibility will build up one person, and break down another.

The 'how' of change, as I say, often baffles me. There are only a few rules which I think I have recognized over the years. One is that there is no set formula for producing a change in people. Each is an individual and needs individual consideration. Another is that, basically, no one person can change another. Change has to come from inside a person. All you can do about it is perhaps to prepare the way, to provide a situation, even to present a choice. Change requires an act of will that cannot be sub-contracted to someone else; and, if it is to be genuine and effective, it needs to take place free of outside pressure.

I am no theologian, but I do know that Christians believe change comes from the entry of the Spirit of God, and His dwelling within the person, to make change permanent. Others may describe the process in other terms. However one describes it is not so important as whether one experiences it. This can be done without being able to analyse the process, as indeed happened to me. I responded to the possibility of change in certain well-established areas of failure in my own life, and to the vision that a similar change, passed from man to man on a big scale, could alter the world. And I found that it worked in my life.

Looking back over the years, I think I can add two other rules on the question of what changes people. One is to expect anything to happen, even miracles; the other is the reverse of the same coin —to have endless patience. A third might be : 'If change doesn't happen in other people in a situation, it may have to begin with oneself.'

An example of this is a story against himself told by Dick Cosens, a man I used to find difficult to get on with, but with whom I now have, I think, a genuine understanding. He is a broad-shouldered muscular shop steward, a fitter at Hawker-Siddeley's aircraft factory near London. He says that he only makes one or two small parts; but if you leave them out the aero-plane falls out of the sky. When he shakes hands with you, he seems deliberately to soften his grip, but despite this it makes my knuckles crack. Some few years ago he was one of those who initiated the group I referred to earlier, who set out to promote

unity between the British and French aerospace industries. Their
first move was to send a small party of trade unionists to Toulouse
to meet the union leaders in Sud Aviation, then working on plans
for Concorde and other projects with very uncertain futures.

The British found themselves facing a much larger group of
Frenchmen, who showed more hostility than enthusiasm for the
encounter. In fact, the opening remark was : 'Why is it that you
British are so big-headed, and think you are the only people who
can build aeroplanes?' Cosens felt his temperature rising; but,
realizing that the point was crucial to their mission, he took hold
of himself, thought hard, and then said : 'I am sorry. You are
quite right. We are big-headed, and we have thought that we are
the only people who can build aeroplanes.' The spokesman relaxed
and pounded him on the shoulder; frowns were replaced by
smiles, and the discussion went vigorously and positively ahead.

It was the first of many moves which also involved top management, the two governments, television and the press. Whatever one's views on Concorde, the European air-bus, and other
international projects, the gain in better Franco-British relations
has been undeniable.

As to unexpected change, here are two contrasting stories from
my own experience.

At a big occasion, a man accosted me and said : 'Do you
remember me?' I looked at him closely, and replied that I could
not remember ever meeting him before. He said that he was in
business in the Midlands, and that we had met at a meeting held
after business hours in a café near London Bridge. Bill Jaeger,
now an internationally known figure in labour and industry, had
been in the chair. The occasion he mentioned was some twenty
years in the past, and I had taken part in many such affairs in
many places. I did remember that meeting, but I could not con-
nect this man with it. 'We had a talk after the meeting,' he went
on, 'and I made with you my first attempt at listening for guidance from God. You asked me if I had any thoughts, and I
said no. You then said that you believed I had some thought, but
it was something I was unwilling to face. I denied it.' He continued : 'You were right, of course. I had been keeping two sets
of books in my business, to deceive the tax people, and the thought
I had was to go to them and tell them this. When I got back

home, I eventually did it. I escaped prosecution—I don't know how. I paid what was due, and my whole life has been on different lines ever since. I just wanted to thank you.'

The odd thing was that I still remembered nothing at all about it. It could hardly be an invented story. Apparently both he and I had thoughts which were something more than human wisdom, in those few minutes of quiet which he described. And it had changed the course of his whole life.

Stanley R., on the staff of a marine insurance company in London, was a central figure in the other experience. An office colleague of his had talked with him about Moral Re-Armament, and brought him to supper with my wife and me in the early part of 1940, at our home in Walton-on-Thames. I have rarely been so repelled by any person. Short, stocky, and awkward, he was a chain-smoker, scattering tobacco ash liberally over the carpets and furnishings. He had a permanent chip on his shoulder, contradicted anything one said in a very rude way, and pronounced what I considered to be very stupid opinions on every possible subject. He seemed the classic example of a bore, so aptly defined as 'a man who talks about himself when you want to talk about yourself'. Perhaps my antagonism came from our being too much alike.

He was also very good at getting his own way, for by the end of the evening we found that we had invited him, his wife and daughter for lunch on the following Sunday. The reason was that, despite the difficulties of conversation with such a man, we had convinced him that Moral Re-armament was the one thing most needed—by his wife.

Their daughter was about the age of our five-year-old Brian. When the three arrived, the two children disappeared into the garden, possibly pursued (I cannot now remember) by Brian's 1½-year-old sister. Stanley, managing as ever, took me off for a walk, leaving the women together in the kitchen.

I asked Constance later if they had talked at all of how people could change, but she said, 'No. I had no guidance to bring it up.' They had talked comfortably of children, cooking recipes, Winifred's uncertain health, and so on. We heard afterwards that she had come to Walton in a state of terror that she would be pressed to do something to produce change in her life. When

FROM MAN TO MAN

it did not happen, she was so relieved that her heart opened, the
new spirit began to enter, and change began. It impressed Stanley
so much that he began to change too.

What started then was solid and real enough to have lasted,
so far, for thirty-six years, constantly refreshed by daily times of
listening in the early morning. Stanley did not become a super-
man overnight, a Napoleon of the business world or anything
like that. He remained a fairly middle-grade office worker. The
big and obvious difference was that the new Stanley really cared
for other people both in the office and out. The change was so
marked that I have never seen him without myself experiencing
a lift of faith and hope.

As to the essential quality of patience, I have been most impressed by the way certain people have been patient with me.
Christopher Prescott, for example, has been a true friend for
forty years. When I first knew him, he was working for Thos.
Cook & Son, the travel agents. He left them and, after strenuous
training for it, decided to work without pay for Moral Re-
Armament for the rest of his life. I am one of countless people
in many countries who owe much to him.

He was one of a large family, including several well-known
Rugby footballers among his brothers, one of whom served as
secretary to the governing body of the sport. Kit, however, was
a rowing man at Oxford. He blinked at the world through glasses
thicker than mine, and in addition is colour-blind. In his youth,
owing to this, he went to a dance in full evening dress, and scarlet
socks. Later, his wife had to tell him what tie to wear, and drove
him, for he could not discern the colour of traffic lights. If he
had played Rugby, he might well have found himself pulling down
a man wearing the wrong colours.

It was hard to define what he gave me over the years. 'Caring'
is too diffuse and soft a word. His attitude was robust in the
extreme, but never overbearing. If I did not respond, it in no
way affected his attitude. Sometimes it has just been a matter
of keeping in touch, and it was uncanny how often greetings cards
have come through the door on my actual birthday, or on a
wedding anniversary, despatched perhaps from Australia, Jamaica
or Rhodesia.

Once or twice, I have had a letter saying, 'I was thinking of writing to Blank, suggesting such and such, when it struck me that it might come better from you. What do you think?' Many times, he has showed a greater faith in my possibilities than I have in myself. Once, when I was very depressed by moral defeat, he said : 'I don't worry much about your failures. They are child-ish things. What interests me much more is the creative and new things you initiate so often.' Did I? Another time, as we said goodbye after he and Joyce his wife had spent a weekend with us and the children, he said to me with a grin : 'Whatever we think of you, old chap, the kids are tops.'

At one period, he and his wife lived with us for a year or more. It was strenuous, particularly the evening when we cele-brated his fifty-fifth birthday by having sixty people to supper. It was, however, a daily lesson on how his tough and sometimes erratic personality could be tamed and re-directed into a broad current of creative activity for the good of a vast range of people. The telephone bill went up sharply. Every day something seemed to happen, some person be contacted, which widened our horizons and made us think afresh of the positive possibilities of change in the world.

Kit's attitude has shown another aspect of what Dr Buchman called 'life-changing', the art of giving faith to others. It is not a question of imposing something on people, but of releasing possi-bilities for good which are already there.

Others have given us similar faithfulness. One especially needs to be mentioned, for of all my City friends he probably still means most, although it is years since cancer took him. Harold Lindley was an average adjuster, helping shipowners and cargo owners to present their claims on their insurers. Our regular lunches together were usually short and simple. At one time the place was always the smoking-room of the Great Eastern Hotel, and his choice was automatically brought by his favourite waiter—very ripe Gorgonzola cheese, wholemeal biscuits, a slice of cherry cake, and a pot of coffee. The fact that Harold was patient with me was clean against his nature. Genial though he could be, there were many times when his mouth tightened over our discussions.

They included every aspect of life. He rebuked me for sloppi-ness in dress, saying that it showed a lack of respect for other people. His own shoes always had a gloss greater than anyone's, a gloss invariably heightened with a duster before he left the office for lunch. Yet when, later in life, he sometimes came to the City in tweeds and brown shoes, and I teased him on it, he said : 'When you reach my age, you also will be allowed a little eccentricity.' On the other hand, when I once told him hesitantly of how Bible reading had affected me, he was very serious, and said that kind of experience was the very core of life. His knowledge of marine insurance, when I consulted him professionally, saved my firm from paying thousands of pounds in dud claims. But when he thought I had short-paid a shipowner by £5 on a claim, his indignation was tremendous. I think his views on the point were wrong (and I stuck to my decision), but the honesty of his indignation was real enough. Most of all I remember him, the sun-browned face and the slim upright figure, as a man who turned neither right nor left, but went straight on, and expected me to do the same.

Perhaps I should touch on a point which seems to matter to a lot of people. I am always being asked why I do not take alcoholic drinks, or serve them at home. People seem to think there is a rule about it in Moral Re-Armament circles. This is not the case. Rules are not the issue.

With me, the issue arose some time after I started trying to live by absolute standards. I was never a heavy drinker. I enjoyed an occasional glass, and I can even remember one or two occasions when perhaps I was a little unsure of the control of my feet. I never, however, reached the state of the gentleman who owlishly watched an electric fan for a long period, before observing : 'Clock's fast.'

What made me think seriously about it was the effect which heavy drinking was having on two of the people with whom I sometimes had a friendly glass. They were men very close to me in different ways, and I felt that both health and character were being affected.

I got so concerned about it that I discussed it one evening with a friend, Tom Shillington, a red-haired Irishman who was to die in the Western Desert not too long afterwards, killed by a shell as he tried to help a friend out of a burning tank at El Alamein. I told him that I had a vague feeling that, every time I took a drink with either of these friends, it helped them down a slope from which they might not recover. Tom suggested time to listen for guidance. After it, I hesitantly said that I wondered if I should try giving it up for a month. Tom exploded—he was a gay and volatile fellow, but basically very serious—with the words, 'That doesn't sound to me like a revolutionary decision!' I admitted that my real thought had been just, 'Give it up'. Apart from the fact that this occurred just as I was beginning to appreciate French wines, I have never regretted doing so.

Unfortunately, it was too late to help the two unfortunates. Both died prematurely, one of them after a broken marriage and losing his job. This was no reason, however, for going back on the decision. I regard it as unimportant whether one modestly enjoys alcohol or not; but it is extremely important what controls one's decisions. If it is impossible for a person to do without alcohol, or if friendships depend on mutual indulgence in it, then a very clear moral issue arises.

Sometimes, I get from abstinence unexpected dividends in the form of amusement. On one occasion I spent some hours in hard negotiation with a man noted for his talents in this field—a high Communist functionary, as it happens. He and his colleagues tried every device on me and my companions. At one point, he brought out bottles of wine and glasses. I refused. 'Why not?' he asked. 'Are you a Muslim or something?'

Shamelessly borrowing a reason used by another man in like circumstances, I said: 'No. It's just that I like a clear head in dealing with a man like you.' He held up a brimming glass, and retorted: 'Well, I need some encouragement when I'm dealing with a man like you.' He won the point, but we won the negotiation, collecting 98 per cent of what we wanted. It was some £80,000. And the next time we met, he offered me coffee. Good coffee it was, too.

The real point of change in the individual is not the change in the individual, but what may flow from it. Certainly, it should make the individual a better worker, manager, teacher, wife or husband. Should it not also release a moral ideological force into society? I feel sure it should. When the world is so much in need of change, anyone who finds how it can happen can hardly keep it to himself. In fact, it is not possible to keep it to oneself. People talk about it.

Once I heard a Japanese say that he first heard about Moral Re-Armament in Russia, where he was a prisoner of war. The prisoners were given systematic training, with a view to making them convinced communists, and the course included an assessment and condemnation of this alternative ideology. It made him want to investigate it when he returned to Japan.

One serio-comic experience affecting myself involved a certain shipowner who frequently wrote abusive letters to my firm, even though we were supposed to be acting for and protecting him. He had reduced several of my colleagues to utter frustration, so much so that some refused to deal with him. I think he must have had a blind spot, and was quite unaware of the import of these letters or of their effect on the recipients. Maybe it was a sort of eruption from his subconscious mind. I dealt with a fairly serious claim against one of his ships. As my file grew, his letters to me got ruder and more violent in expression. I tried to correct him, soothe him, anything. Eventually, I got such a letter that I thought a frontal counter-attack was the only honourable course. I sent the letter back with one addressed personally to him enclosing it. This said that his statements were untrue, and that I thought it undesirable in his or our interests for the letter to remain on file. I asked him to destroy both the original and his copy.

He came back with a personal letter in some indignation, not so much because (he said) I had misinterpreted his statements, but because he was so treated by a man who was much concerned about the future of the world, or words to that effect. I don't know where he got that opinion of me, as my own contacts with him had always been entirely formal and technical. Someone must have told him of my convictions. In any case, he stopped sending me rude letters.

How one spreads ideas depends, I suppose, on one's own bent, as well as on one's own circumstances. In a busy City office, there is not much time for philosophical or ideological discussion. There are occasionally times when this is appropriate; but one may have to rely more on the seeds being spread by the wind, as in the instance cited above. Often, it is a question of taking the opportunities which people give, answering the questions they ask, even inviting them to participate in this and that activity which may appeal to them. Flexibility of approach is essential. In my time, I have

N

occasionally erred by way of over-enthusiasm, filling unwilling ears with inadvisable speeches. Perhaps now I am too hesitant, sometimes. Often, the unspoken word is the most effective. Who was it who said, 'The way you act speaks so loudly that I cannot hear what you say'?

Whatever the tactics, there needs to be behind whatever one does a steady purpose. Many of us flinch from the concept of ideology—a code of ideas which affects every detail of one's life, and which one burns to see dominant throughout the world. We sometimes get glimpses of what an ideology is, often in a negative form, the Fascism and Nazism of yesterday, the Communism of today. Because we dislike it and perhaps do not understand it, we pretend it does not exist, instead of aiming to secure the supremacy of a positive alternative.

Philosophy, passion and plan are said to be the essentials of a true ideology. St Paul had such an ideology; so did Francis of Assisi.

In Canada in 1975 we heard how a few months earlier the port of Vancouver had been completely immobilized by a strike, beginning with the grain handlers. What puzzled many people was that the strike continued long after the employers had agreed the terms of a settlement. Two different sources, both from the heart of the shipping industry, gave me the same reason for this odd development. It is well known that Communist influences are strong in the harbour unions on the West Coast of North America. The word had gone out, it was said, that Vancouver must be kept closed, so that one particular ship, carrying an aid cargo of wheat, could not sail for Bangladesh. Then it could be said throughout Asia that 'capitalist' Canada made promises, but did not keep them. People might starve in the deltas of Bengal and scores of ships could lie idle, just to score an ideological victory. I cannot give legal proof. Who could? But sober men accepted this as true.

Again, I watched in Dublin an interview on Irish television with a leader of Sinn Fein usually described as the political branch of the Irish Republican Army. It is now generally accepted that the I.R.A. is deeply infiltrated by international left-wing revolutionaries. The interviewer asked, 'How does it help your campaign for a united Ireland to burn shops and factories in the North?' The reply was, 'Whether it helps that campaign or not, it is certainly a step towards the destruction of the corrupt capitalist society.' That again illustrates ideology.

A little honest contemplation of any newspaper's headlines will reveal other examples where ideological aims are daringly and expertly pursued by certain elements, sometimes openly, more often under disguise.

The real issue is whether people equally committed to a constructive ideology, based on caring for all, can be more effective and more determined than those who will ruthlessly destroy in order to bring about the victory of their concepts.

I was in India when I heard of the death of Peter Howard. An Indian journalist told me that during the preceding months many in Kerala in South India had received letters from Howard —social workers, teachers, politicians. It was a time of great economic and political trouble in that area. The letters were short, their usual content amounting to : 'I am so sorry to read of your difficulties. Is there anything which I can do to help?' They had made a deep impression, and encouraged many to take positive action. Yet Howard at the time was engaged in a strenuous tour of South America, speaking to meetings of many thousands, meeting heads of state, students, dockers, all kinds of people. To care at the same time what happened in Kerala, that again was ideology.

William Jaeger, whom I mentioned earlier, is another example. When I first met him, he was still at college, and it was then that he first had a clear conception of his calling. Coming from a working-class background at Stockport, near Manchester, he felt that his task should be to develop the positive, creative purpose in the world of labour. A phrase of Dr Buchman's which gripped him was 'Labour led by God can lead the world'. As years went on, he found that this was in no way a plan confined to a class. Management was equally a part, also government, those involved in the race issue, and so on.

His appetite for human contacts is inexhaustible. The first stage of his life's work was in East London, and the basis of it was a list of names, the members of all the local councils throughout East London, birthplace of the British Labour movement. There were 700 men and women on the list. Bill and his few colleagues saw all of them, as a start.

Later, he worked for several years in the United States. During this, with a small group, he attended a number of national trade union conferences. One of his closest associates, Duncan Corcoran, a former shipyard worker from the Clyde, told me once that before one of these conferences Jaeger and the others checked the list of 1,800 delegates and found that between them they had already met 1,200 of them.

In recent years he has regularly attended sessions of the International Labour Organization in Geneva. After one such visit, he lunched in the City with me and a well-known banker, and told us about those weeks. He had talked with 250 delegates, about a quarter of whom he mentioned by name during the lunch, and quoted from the conversations with many of them. As we parted, the banker said to him : 'If I can help, I'd be glad to work with you at any time.' And a number of times he has.

What is his work? Partly, to my mind anyway, it is to do with people and their problems. A business man from Australia told me he discussed the future of his business with Jaeger, who said bluntly : 'To begin with, you should break with that partner of yours. He's a crook.' The business man refused to believe it—until after the partner had swindled him. A chastened man, he has now got his business on a better footing.

If he visits a city, Jaeger thinks nothing of fixing an interview every hour with people of all kinds, and enlists any friends available to help. I went with him on some interviews in 1975, one of them with a very left-wing Labour leader. Bill gave him news of mutual friends, summarized his own background (and mine) in two or three sentences, and got down to discussing fact and principle of local and world issues. After half an hour the union leader said : 'I agree with you on one point. When we sit down with management, there is selfishness on both sides of the table.' To reach that point with a hard-line Communist in half an hour was, I thought, brisk going. It illustrates the other side of his work, too, a concern for the climate of thinking in the world.

In the United States, lunching with business friends, I quoted Jaeger on his concern for Anglo-American relations, saying that he had been told by a U.S. official in Europe that in 1974 Britain had sent twenty-four trade union delegations to Moscow, and only one to Washington. One of my friends noted this on the back of an envelope, saying : 'I'm seeing President Ford on Tuesday. I'll try to tell him that, for I am sure he doesn't want British and American labour to drift apart.'

Jaeger is realistic, indeed modest, about his work. One evening he had some friends of ours asking questions for two or three hours about what he and others were doing in different countries. But he summed it up by saying : 'We do what we can. And if we have to do it all over again in five or ten years' time, we will.'

I know others who have pursued with the same single-mindedness their conviction as to what needs to be done. One is a diplomat who has made sincere friends in capitalist countries, in the Communist bloc, and in the Third World, and has had a share in developing policies which on certain issues have united all three groups. Another is a business man, based on Australia, who has applied moral standards in industrial matters in ways which have significantly improved nutrition in several Asian countries. Such tasks take years, and the building of constructive relationships on a big scale. It has also needed the daily practice of listening thoughtfully to the voice within, and absolute loyalty to whatever moves are seen as necessary, large or small. These men, like Howard, Jaeger, Cosens, Frits Philips, and many others, demonstrate an ideology, and a determination that the world shall be different.

Another of Will Rogers' dry jokes was : 'God made man a little lower than the angels, and he's been getting a little lower ever since.' But we don't have to take that as a serious summary of mankind's destiny.

Index

Index